Cycling

Through

Depression

Ed Bradley

ISBN: 098910740X
ISBN 13: 9780989107402

Library of Congress Control Number: 2013904990
CreateSpace Independent Publishing Platform
North Charleston, South Carolina

*This book is dedicated to my daughters, Shannon, Erin, and Jenny.
You have made the world a better place since the day you arrived.*

Special Thanks

The number of people who made this trip and book possible is enormous. I received so much support from so many individuals. I apologize to anyone I have left out. The following list is in no particular order.

Rose Bradley, Jessica Cushman, Bob and Mary Noble, Nicky Noble, Bobby Noble, Kim Noble, Bradley Teribury, Joel and Jessica Teribury, Lauren Teribury, Kate and Doug Shifflett, Haley Shifflett, John and Robin Winkler, Gerry and Judy Mittica, Carissa Mittica, Jane Mortenson, Joe and Michelle Kane, Tim and Gail Gardner, Meredith Tips-McLaine, Alison Bromell, Harry and Terry Linnemeyer, Ann and Phil Jones, Faye (Jacksonville, Florida), Jimmy and Mernagh Howze, Kale Poland, Cindy Ballantyne, Bob Brown, Katherine Silta, Barb Guli, Sue Pollard, Kelly and Jim Tully, Chuck and Connie Joffrion, Ben and Jeanie Hart, Michelle and Jim Jardine, Renee Jardine, Eliz and Jess Jardine, Mike Miller, Jay and Maureen Cusak, Duangjai Jeradechakul, Jim Sands, Charlie Hartz, Michelle McMillen, Adventure Cycling, Ann Perham, Mary Perham, Nico, Rich and Eileen Wuerthele, Chris Miller, Tom Johnson, Katie Marvel and Brandy Marie.

Special Acknowledgments

Pat Fasano, I miss you every day. You left way too soon.

Ted Bundy, I wish I had known how much pain you were in.

Lyrics to "Hollow Man" used by permission of the writer, Mike Miller.

CHAPTER ONE

What Came Before

LEAVING HOME

June 23, 2010 Springfield, Vermont

Today I drove away from my life. It wasn't a perfect life, but it was one I never dreamt I would leave. My daughters, Erin and Jenny, helped me pack the van, took some pictures, and waved goodbye.

Did they cry? I can't remember. My sadness enveloped me completely; I was swaddled in it. In an odd way, the sadness was comfortable. Enjoyable? No, but it was what I had become used to; sadness had been my constant companion for some time. We were like two broken-down barflies, commiserating at an end-of-the-world dive bar. We really didn't like each other, but we had no one else to turn to. So sadness and I did another shot of rotgut tequila, waited, and hoped for the blackout.

My life had been a house of cards, probably for much longer than I was aware of. When the first breezes made it tremble, I was in denial. Even after the gale-force wind hit the house, collapsing it on top of me; I don't think I understood that it was over. I lay in the rubble, broken. I was hoping for it to be a bad dream, wishing I could rebuild the house, praying for rescue—but rescue never came.

My marriage of twenty-four years was over. I was broken-hearted, not like a country-western song, but like an apocalypse. I wasn't the first person to go through this, but that didn't matter. In my head I knew I would come out in the end whole, or semi-whole, but my heart didn't believe it. It didn't want to come out at the other end of it; it wanted it never to have happened. To me it was the end of the universe, the apocalypse, Armageddon, and Ragnarök all rolled into one.

My job of twenty years had been a source of pride, a place where I had made a difference every day. That had collapsed on me also. Now it was a place where I felt like a character in a *Dilbert* strip. I had become a drone, a piece of the furniture. I had migraines, acid reflux, backaches, knee aches, and insomnia. When I did fall asleep, I had dreams. Dreams that were unbearable, not because they were nightmares; they were unbearable because they were wonderful. In these dreams Nan and I were happy. When I awoke, I wept—not a great way to start a day.

Then one day I was just done with my job; it held nothing for me but misery. It was time for me to go, to move on, to "hit the road, Jack" and not come back. I was surprised how effortless it was to leave a job of twenty years, to leave a hospital I loved. It was as if a light switch had been turned off. No mess, no fuss, *no mas*—the light was turned off. I was like Lot; I never looked back.

Leaving the hospital was the second sanest decision I made in 2010. The sanest was when I decided to take a long bicycle trip—from Fort Kent, Maine, to Key West, Florida, on US Route 1

That's where I was headed when I drove away from my daughters and my house.

I was headed for the journey, the adventure of my life. I might have known it then, but I didn't feel it yet.

WHY I TOOK THIS TRIP

It became clear to me that my life as I knew it was coming to an end. I was having a difficult time getting my mind around that concept. I really didn't want to start a new life at fifty-three, but this one was over. In my mind I started to try on new lives. Joining the Peace Corps, building houses in Haiti, becoming a math or science teacher, and teaching English in Thailand were a few things that auditioned for the part of Ed's second life. All of them had their own appeal, but they weren't what I needed right now.

I always had fantasized about taking a long physical trip. The idea of a walkabout was very appealing. I wanted something that would challenge me mentally and physically—something to test my limits. I needed to take a journey to test my assumptions about the world and myself.

Bicycling came to mind; I had mountain-biked on and off for several years—nothing extreme, just short rides near my home. The longest trip was less than thirty miles. Nan and I also had taken the girls on several bike rides while we were on vacation. We had ridden the Cape Code rail trail. We also had explored the carriage roads in Acadia National Park multiple times. I remember feeling real joy on those rides. The physical act of biking was comfortable to me; the motion of the bike under me felt right. The pace of a trip also appealed to me. It was slow enough to see the world as I passed through it but fast enough to cover some miles. When I finally settled on a bicycle trip, the next question was "Where?"

I considered Australia, especially since I had dreamed about going there for many years. Australians speak English and have a reputation for being a friendly, fun-loving people. There was a great deal of information on the Internet about biking there as well; it was a very appealing idea. While I was researching Australia, I stumbled on the site of an Australian cyclist who had biked in Southeast Asia. He made it sound wonderful. The mix of different cultures and the exotic look of the landscape spoke to me; it felt like it would be an amazing adventure. I was very close to making this trip happen. However, staying in the United States also was very appealing. I had a longtime fascination with US Route 1, and I liked the idea of being near the ocean for large portions of the trip. Maybe I was a bit of a wimp also; being on the East Coast would keep me within reasonable distances of family and friends. Staying in my own country also gave me the safety net I needed to begin the trip.

FINANCIAL CONSIDERATIONS

Once I was done with my old life I made the decision to simplify my new life. I reduced my monthly bills to as close to zero as possible. Nan bought me out of the house, which left me a small nest egg (road egg?) for the trip. We split up our vehicles; I took the van and the Saab. Both of these were paid for. I sold both of them. No more car repair bills, no more car insurance, and no more gasoline to pay for. When I left Vermont I was homeless, that meant no mortgage payment, no electric bill, and no oil bill. My monthly bills when I left were; $25 dollar for internet access for my I-Pad, and $50 for my cell phone. Money goes a long way when your fixed costs are under $100 a month.

WHAT DID EVERYONE THINK?

When I announced my decision to take this trip the decision was overwhelmingly positive. Nan told me she thought the idea was brilliant. The first and only time I heard her use that word. My daughters were also proud and excited. My friends shook their collective head and bombarded me with questions. Where will you sleep? What will you eat? Are you going to carry a gun? Are you afraid of animals? What will you do if it rains? And the ones that deemed the most important; how will we know where you are and if you are safe.

In response to the last two questions I started a Facebook page for the trip; Cycling Through Depression. The name struck me as the perfect name for the trip. I had been cycling through the ups and downs of depression for years. Now I was going to make a physical journey through my depression. The page became my life line to my friends and family, my journal, my therapist and the basis for this book.

THE DEPRESSION

My depression was diagnosed when I was in my forties. To be honest it wasn't so much diagnosed; rather I finally admitted it. I had known I was depressed for a long time, but I was embarrassed and ashamed to admit it. It struck me as a personal failure, a character flaw. When the darkness came over me, I felt I should just be able to overcome it. I should be able to will myself out of depression. I had days when I got home from work when I could do nothing except lie on the couch. Hating myself became a full-time job at times. I thought I was just lazy when I couldn't face mowing the lawn. Often on the weekends, I'd lie down on the living room floor and fall asleep. Sleep was my escape from my depression. If I didn't have to go to work, I couldn't face getting up in the morning.

I wasn't depressed like Eeyore from *Winnie the Pooh*. I didn't mope around with a dark cloud over my head, sighing and telling everyone how sad I was. Most people never would have guessed I was depressed; I held a good job and raised a family.

When I finally admitted it, I sought help. My physician pre-scribed an antidepressant that helped me a great deal. But I still struggled. My dream was that this bike trip would help with my depression. I also hoped it would raise awareness of depression as an illness.

THE BIKE AND THE TRAILER

I spent a long time researching bicycles. Almost any bike can be used for touring. Mountain, road, recumbent, hybrid, fixed-gear—you probably could do it on a unicycle. After much research, I settled on the Surly Long Haul Trucker. I liked the solid-steel frame, the slightly wider tires, and the bike's overall ruggedness. In the end I think it was the name that sealed the deal; the Long Haul Trucker is just a great name. Surly has the best names for bikes—they also make the Karate Monkey, the Pugsley, and the Big Dummy.

I also spent some time deciding between panniers or a trailer. Both have their pros and cons. After I'd read information on various online forums, the debate appeared to be almost religious in nature. In the end I went with the B.O.B. trailer. I liked the idea of keeping as much equipment off the bike as possible. Ultimately I think the name was the deciding factor. How can you not love "The Beast of Burden"?

THE TRIP NORTH

The van I drove to Maine was a wreck. The driver's side door didn't open, and the automatic windows didn't work. The panel for the door on the driver's side was gone. Some of the lights on the dash worked; others didn't. The sliding door on the rear passenger side was permanently stuck shut. One headlight pointed a little up, the other a little down and to the side. The radio worked a minor miracle. The van had been the first luxury vehicle Nan and I had purchased: sliding power doors, automatic windows, backup alarm, DVD player (we didn't even have one in the house then!), leather-wrapped steering wheel, and a six-CD—count them, six—, CD player. It was like we had won the lottery.

Now the poor girl was limping along, and I was asking her to do one last trip, her last hurrah—a sojourn of five hundred miles north, past Bangor, Maine, to Fort Kent, Maine, her final resting place, where she would be allowed to retire peacefully.

June 24, 2010

When I arrived at 1:30 a.m. at the Northern Door Inn, the only motel in Fort Kent, I received some bad news. They were sold out! How could they be sold out on a Thursday? A big family reunion was taking place. I was tired — like a dog that had been beaten all day then put in the basement for the night. Tired and with nowhere to stay, I received the first of many kindnesses during my trip. The night clerk let me sleep on the couch. I had to be up at 5:00 a.m., but it was better than sleeping in the van. Five in the morning came very quickly. Wiping the sleep out of my eyes, I started the day. The weather was overcast, with rain in the forecast. The first thing I need to do was buy a few things for the trip — boring stuff like toothpaste, soap, and sunscreen, and, yes, a helmet. I had to drive the twenty-odd miles east to the nearest Kmart, in Madawaska, Maine, to make my purchases. Then I had to retrace my route to Fort Kent and head south to Eagle Lake. Amazingly I had been unable to find anyone in Fort Kent who wanted the van for free. I found a garage in Eagle Lake that would buy it. I sold the van for a hundred dollars and found a space to hitch my trailer up to the bike. As insane as it sounds, I never had ridden the bike with the trailer attached, and I never had attached the trailer to the bike. I managed to get the trailer securely attached — or so I thought — to the bike. I put on my rain jacket, which was too small, and set off again for Fort Kent in the pouring rain. Feeling pretty proud of myself, I pedaled away from the garage, but pride always comes before the fall. The road was torn up for construction. Between the rain and the road conditions, I wasn't making great time. After about five miles, the back tire froze, and the whole caravan came to a screaming halt. I had installed a piece of the trailer ass backward, and the rear tire had come out of the drop-in. Looking back at the intermediate biker I've become (I doubt I ever will feel like an advanced biker), I can laugh at that idiot at the side of the road. During that moment, however, the last thing I was doing was laughing. Surprisingly I wasn't crying either. I knew no one was coming to rescue me. It was up to me to figure out how to fix this, or my trip would be over before it even had started. Mr. Fixit (a name no one ever has called me) went to work. The rain was pummeling me, making it hard for me to see. The incline I was working on felt like it was at least forty-five degrees. My three-dollar reading glasses kept fogging up and falling off. Half the time I was working almost by touch alone. Finally I managed to get the trailer and the tire apart and then get the rear tire back on. While I was working on this, I had several back spasms that didn't quite drop me to the ground. Eventually I hooked the trailer back on. Several hundred miles later, I'd find out I had left out a few parts, but it would hold until then. As I finished up, I looked down; I was standing in poison ivy. My trip was off to a stunning start. Still a smile came to my face; I had rescued myself. Drenched not to the skin, but to my internal organs, I started back to Fort Kent. When I got back, I went to the motel and got a real room this time. I spent the next few hours drying out my clothes and belongings. I hung everything with me from whatever I could find in the room so that it could dry.

Then, feeling like a veteran biker of one day, I went to Rock's Family Diner for a couple of burgers. My daughter Erin's boyfriend, Adam, had recommended the place. As I sat waiting for my food, I listened to the conversations around me. Fort Kent sits right on the Canadian border and has a very large French-speaking population. Two men sat at the counter conversing in French; then I realized one had switch to English. They continued to speak—one in French, one in English. Then they were both speaking in English. The conversation flowed back and forth, seamlessly, between French and English.

When I returned to the motel room, I felt stiff and tired. My back was sore, my right knee swollen. Still I was happy to be on my journey. Fatigue finally overcame me. I couldn't even stay awake for the first pitch of the Red Sox game.

CHAPTER TWO

Maine

Day One; June 25, 2010
Fort Kent, Maine, to Cyr Plantatio,
Maine—Fifty Miles

Today felt like the true start of the trip; I would be headed to Key West, Florida. Getting up, however, was a challenge. I felt stiff all over. I couldn't raise my leg over the crossbar of the bike; I had to balance the bike and myself and use my hands to throw my leg over. As the day wore on, my body grudgingly loosened up. My plan for the day was to get to Van Buren, Maine, which was about fifty miles away. That was pretty ambitious for me. The longest distance I had covered in a day was less than thirty miles. Pulling the trailer proved to be a real challenge. Actions that had been trivial without the trailer, such as reaching for my water bottle, became a daredevil adventure. Shifting became Greek astrophysics. Rolling hills became rolling hells; a gentle zephyr in my face became a tsunami of terror. Stopping and resting constantly was the soup of the day. Physically it was a tough day; mentally it was awesome. It was sunny and clear. The sun felt wonderful on my skin, and it I felt great to be alive. I hadn't felt this good in a long, long time. Across the river from me was Canada; in front of me was US Route 1, which runs all the way to Key West. I felt like I was going from one end of the world to the other. Every few miles there were border crossings, followed by WELCOME TO MAINE signs. Kids ran to the edge of the road to yell, "Nice bike!" and "Where are you going?" Apparently I was the local entertainment for the weekend.

When I reached Van Buren, Maine, I felt tremendous. There was a small hotel, which looked appealing after my first real day of biking. There was some light left in the day, and I decided to push on. The next couple of hills were very rough on me. Very soon I started to think about the hotel I had passed up. For a fleeting moment I thought of turning back, but I couldn't bear to backtrack on my first day. Twilight set in, and I was getting really tired. I stopped on the shoulder and gazed up another hill. It looked overwhelming. I questioned the sanity of putting in so many miles on the first day. Then I questioned the sanity of the whole trip. While I was resting, a young boy, maybe ten, biked up to me and asked if I was OK. I asked him if there was any place to camp nearby, and he said there was an abandoned hunting camp at the top of the hill. He also told me there was an ATV club just across the road from it that had a water pump I could use to fill my water bottles.

Feeling a little jolt of energy, I followed my Northern Maine guide up the hill. The hunting camp was the perfect place to set up my tent. The ground was flat, and I'd be completely hidden from the road. I set up my tent in the fading light for the first time. It proved to be a small challenge. While I was setting up for the night, my new friend entertained himself with my iPad. He then seemed to come to a sudden realization. Being in the woods with a full-grown man he had met just a few minutes ago might not be the brightest idea he'd ever had. He handed me my iPad and said he should let his parents know where he was. Then he pedaled away down the hill. I was afraid I'd get a visit from a concerned father or the police that evening.

The night was beautiful, with a clear sky and tons of brilliant stars to look at. I talked with Nan on the phone. It was still hard for me to believe that we would soon be divorced. It was a true blessing to be so tired. I was too tired to be sad; I drifted off to sleep beneath the Maine sky. The first day of my journey was over.

Day Two; June 26, 2010

Cyr Plantation, Maine, to Presque Isle,

Maine—Thirty Miles

I awoke in the middle of the night to a light but persistent rain. Running around in the dark, I threw the rain fly over the tent. I gathered my belongings as quickly as I could and stowed them in my trailers waterproof bag. I crawled back into the tent and drifted back to sleep. In the morning everything was damp. I felt a little stupid for having left everything exposed to the elements. It was due to a combination of being tired and inexperienced, but fortunately nothing was damaged.

I left Cyr Plantation in good spirits. My body was stiff and sore, but I actually was proud of the discomfort. I felt like I had accomplished something yesterday, and the aches and pains were proof of it. The temperature was warm—not too hot and very pleasant to bike in. I rode through some sprinkles of rain; they felt good on my skin. I stopped at a supermarket in Caribou, Maine, for lunch, where I wolfed down a milkshake in a bottle and a package of deli ham. I saved four green bananas for later. While I ate outside the supermarket, I had two visitors who were very interested in my trip. Like many people I talked to during my trip, they loved my B.O.B. trailer; in fact it was a conversation starter everywhere I went.

After lunch I headed for Presque Isle. When I arrived, I stopped at a bike shop, Mojo Sports, to ask about a cheap motel. When they found out I was on my way to Key West, they went ballistic. They ran out of the store to see my rig, bombarded me with questions, and generally made me feel like a rock star.

They ended up giving me a book, electrolyte powder, and a 20-percent discount on anything I wanted. A young man named Kale Poland jumped on the Internet and immediately joined my Facebook page "Cycling Through Depression." Kale would become both a source of encouragement and inspiration for me. While I was on this trip, he would compete in Mexico in a Quintuple Ironman, where he would swim twelve miles, bike 560 miles, and run 131 miles.

Many times when I didn't think I could do another mile, I'd think of Kale and push on.

Kale and the crew at Mojo directed me to the Northern Lights Motel, where I rented a very clean and comfortable room. I washed my shorts and riding jersey in the sink and managed to get everything dried out from the previous night. I ordered a takeout pizza and wings; I ate half the pizza for dinner and saved the rest for breakfast.

Day Three; June 27, 2010

Presque Isle, Maine, to Houlton,

Maine—Thirty-Seven Miles

I had pizza for breakfast—the breakfast of cross-country bikers. I took it easy today and enjoyed the ride. I stopped at great little town common in Bridgewater, Maine, where I sat in a gazebo and stared at the sky. Farther down the road, I had a great vanilla milkshake in Monticello, where I picked up some deli meat for my evening meal. Early in the day, I saw a model of the planet Jupiter. I didn't think that much about it; I figured it was a school science project. A few miles later, on the other side of the road was a model of Saturn! It was then that I knew I was leaving the solar system. It turned out this stretch of Maine road has the largest representation of the solar system in the world. The models of Jupiter and Saturn are large, about five feet across. The entire model spans forty miles. The Sun is located at University of Maine at Presque Isle. Pluto is in the Houlton Information Center.

I felt strong on the bike today. My legs and arms were adjusting nicely. The rolling hells of yesterday evolved into rolling hecks.

When I arrived in Houlton, I tried to take my bike into Walmart so I could buy a camcorder. I attempted to leave my bike at the customer service` counter but was denied. The bike was deemed a safety hazard. The entire management team followed me as I walked my bike to the exit. At first I thought it was ridiculous. But if guy can put a bomb in his underwear, I guess my bike could contain an alien virus.

The campground I was looking for never materialized, so I stayed at the Ivy Inn. I covered about thirty-seven miles today and a total of 120 miles, according to Google maps.

Day Four; June 28, 2010

Houlton, Maine—Rest Day

I awoke to another light but persistent rain. I felt like somewhat of a sissy, but I made the decision to move up my rest day. I looked at Google maps and found the campground I had missed the night before. I had to backtrack a couple of miles to get to it. When I got there, I found the campground was sparsely inhabited. The owner was glad to see me and threw in free Wi-Fi for the night. My campsite included a covered picnic table. The cover was large enough that I could camp under it and keep my tent out of the rain. I washed my meager belongings and made myself a humble dinner of ramen noodles. I learned a painful lesson today; camping without my family is lonely. I hadn't really camped before I had met Nan. My idea of camping before I'd met her had been staying in a Ramada Inn that was being refurbished at the time. Eventually camping had become a family activity for us. Walking around the campground today felt painfully lonely. I went to bed early and tried not to think about my family.

Day Five; June 29, 2010

Houlton, Maine, to East Grand Lake,

Maine—Forty Two Miles

After two days and one night of camping at My Brother's Campground — which was the name of the campground (I don't have a brother) — I was rested and ready to go. Sleeping in the tent was getting more comfortable. At 5:55 a.m. I woke up. It was raining and cold, so I decided to doze for a while. The next thing I knew, it was 8:00 a.m. When I finally got up, I felt very dizzy. It may have been dehydration, hunger, or my not taking my Paxil. A Coke and a bottle of water later, I was ready to go. I placed my bet on dehydration and vowed to keep a better eye on my fluid intake. After leaving the campground, I went to Tim Horton's, where I had two breakfast wraps and a doughnut; maybe I didn't need the doughnut, but it felt like a decadent treat. I bought a PowerBar at a convenience store and hit the road.

The hills that seemed gentle yesterday had become the Matterhorn. Around noon I stopped for lunch. I picked an idyllic spot to eat—the church steps in a tiny town called Amity in Aroostook County. What could go wrong in a town named Amity? Across the road from church was a picturesque, well-kept cemetery. As I ate lunch, I spotted four people walking up the road. Bits and pieces of their conversation drifted over to me. Two were women; they looked like sisters. The other two were an elderly man and a woman. The elderly couple was telling the history of the family—who was buried where and what they had done with their lives. It was all very Norman Rockwell-like. I crossed the road to speak with them. One of the younger women asked me about my trip and made pleasant small talk. As we were talking, a state police cruiser rolled up. The woman gave me an odd look and said, "I shouldn't be talking with you." Her comment confused me and freaked me out. Two troopers got out of the car. I know that in Vermont troopers ride alone; I assumed they did in rural Maine as well, so it confused me to see two officers get out of the car. Neither one carried himself like a trainee; they both moved with confidence. They came toward me from two angles and appeared to be very focused on me. Maybe I had watched too many episodes of *Law & Order*, but they looked very wary of me. They spoke to the woman first. After a few questions, they dismissed her and the rest of the group. They then questioned me. They were very professional but pointed too. They asked me for my ID; they wanted to know where I had been, where I was going, and why I was here. This wasn't in a chitchat sort of way, and it clearly wasn't a social call. They returned my ID after questioning me and told me, "Good luck." I asked them, "Is there anything I should know?" They responded, "No." As they drove away, two of the women returned and told me that a few days ago a triple homicide had taken place in town. Two men and a ten-year-old boy had been stabbed to death. The assailant hadn't been identified and was still at large. Day five of the trip and I was a person of interest in a triple murder.

I started down the road, a little shaken that I might possibly be sharing the road with a triple murderer. I stopped at a mom-and-pop convenience store, where I got a great pizza for dinner. It started to sprinkle as I was eating my dinner at a picnic table. The sprinkle soon turned into a torrential downpour. The psychopathic murder wandering loose and the pouring rain made my decision easy and guilt free. I found a cabin for the night in a fishing camp called Jami & Bob's Rideout Lodge on East Grand Lake. It was nice to be warm and dry and sleeping in a bed. Having a locked door between the killer and me wasn't bad either. The rustic cabin didn't have a TV, but it was very comfortable. I followed my new ritual of stripping out of my wet clothes, emptying everything out of my bag, and hanging the contents to dry out all over my home for the night. The cabin did feel very home-like, and the weather suddenly the clouds and rain vanished. The world had that feeling of being just right—of being reborn after a storm. Everything had an early-evening glow to it, which took my breath away. I spent some time standing on the dock, looking out over the lake. Just off shore was an island with a very Middle-earth feel. In fact I could almost see the Fellowship of the Ring. I still wasn't feeling right with myself, but I was starting to feel all right with the world. I know that doesn't sound quite right, but it felt right. I had some thoughts that I might be all right in the end, but I was still a long way from being healed.

Day Six; June 30, 2010

Grand Lake, Maine, to North of Calais,

Maine—Fifty-Four Miles

I woke up feeling great. The night at the fishing camp had been wonderful. Jami & Bob's Rideout Lodge had been a perfect stop. I was warm and dry, and so was all my gear. Bob was a great host; he even had given me a safe spot to store my bike the night before. In the morning he spent some time talking with me about the trip. I wonder now if the people in Maine thought I would make it — or did they think I was a crazed man in the middle of a Walter Mitty fantasy? In all fairness, at this point I wasn't sure myself.

I felt like a champ on the bike today. The weather was fantastic, with a few sprinkles, which felt great and was just enough to cool me off. I reached a real milestone during the trip today. I had to pee during the day for the first time on the trip. I'd been pouring fluid into me, but it never was enough. At the end of the day, I was downing water like a drunken sailor guzzling grog after a year at sea. The dam didn't break until thirty minutes after I had stopped for the day. I also did a better job of eating enough. It's very different to think of food as fuel. For so many years, I had taken food for granted. In the past food had been something to be enjoyed, something to be shared with my family. Now it had a much more utilitarian purpose. Its job was to keep me going, to prevent me from passing out in the wilds of Northern Maine. I stopped at a country convenience store for a drink and a rest. While I was sitting inside, I saw a border patrol car drive by. It slowed down and turned around. The officer pulled up and stopped in front of the store, right by my bike. When I came out, he asked where I was going and whether I was an American citizen. I was traveling with my passport, which I produced for him. He looked it over and handed it back. He said the state police had told him I would be coming through. Suddenly I had the feeling that I was an outlaw biker. They were keeping an eye on me; they were pretty sure I wasn't the maniac they were looking for, but apparently they weren't ruling it out. If I was their man, I was escaping at a glacier-like pace. I covered fifty-four miles that day, a new personal record.

Day Seven; July 1, 2010

North of Calais, Maine, to Robbinston,

Maine—Seventeen Miles

I almost broke my head today, sugar bear.

It was another excellent day to bike—not too hot, not too cold, just right. It was a real Goldilocks day. I biked into Calais, a short six miles from where I had slept last night. Calais was the gateway to two great Canadian vacations we'd taken as a family. One was a camping trip to the "home" of Anne of Green Gables, Prince Edward Island. The other was a camping trip to Cape Breton Island, Nova Scotia.

Dissolve to a time long ago—BD (before divorce). The scene was an idyllic country campground, Seal Cove on Prince Edward Island. Our campsite overlooked beautiful Seal Cove. The day we arrived, we were walking on the beach; as we rounded a corner, a flock of herons took flight. To call a group of herons a flock is wholly inadequate; they really are more like a herd. Their cranky prehistoric calls deafened us. In Vermont it's almost statewide news when a single blue heron is spotted; we had just seen a decade's worth. Nan and I looked at each other with those silly grins tourists have when they experience a perfect vacation moment. The twins and Jen were spellbound.

That night as we were in the tent, getting ready for sleep, one of the tent poles slipped. A little annoyed, I unzipped the tent flap and went outside to fix it. As I stood there, shirtless, I heard an almost electric humming, far away at first and then coming closer. That summer had been one of the wettest in Prince Island Edward's history, which meant the mosquito population had risen to record levels, to epic levels, to biblical-plague levels. I didn't know that when I left the tent. I did know very soon that the dinner bell had been rung, and every mosquito on the island had heard it. The buffet was open, and I was it. As I stumbled to the front of the tent, I was a little worried as I swatted at the advancing scouts. That feeling soon escalated to fear and then blind panic as my blood was being drained at an alarming rate. When I reached the flap, I found the door was zipped tightly.

17

As I feverishly tried to get the door open, Nan's sweet voice came from inside the tent. "Just a minute," she said. "I'm getting all the sleeping bags lined up." As I stood there, quickly exsanguinating, envisioning myself becoming a mummified remnant of myself, I started to laugh. When I finally got inside the tent, everyone erupted in laughter. Over the years we've told that story over and over again. The phrase "Just a minute" is still guaranteed to make us all burst into hysterics.

If you want to know what I lost, read that story again. If you want to know the depth of my despair, read that story again.

Maybe I was thinking of this story and wasn't paying attention. My trip almost came to an early and abrupt end. I had used clip-less pedals only a few times before this trip and was no expert in their use. I stopped at a traffic light with my left foot clipped in. When the light turned green, I started to bike. I wobbled, and instinctively, to catch my balance, I placed my hand on the van next to me. Using a family minivan as a point of balance is a very bad idea; toppling over in traffic isn't an experience I'd recommend. As I hit the asphalt, I realized a car wouldn't have to be going very fast to make a squash out of my gourd. The van came to an abrupt stop, and a very nice, panic-stricken woman rushed out to my side. She was sure she had killed or at least maimed me.

Shaken and a little stirred, I stopped at the nearby visitor center to collect myself. The rest of the day, I couldn't stay out of my own way. I banged my shins painfully on the pedals. I knocked the bike over when I stopped for food. I generally acted like I'd never been on a bike before. I couldn't make any headway. At about the twenty-mile mark, I called it quits for the day. I was worried I might somehow kill myself if I didn't get off the bike. I saw a sign for Hillside Campground and decided to stay there for the night. They weren't exaggerating when they had named the campground. It was uphill—mountain-goat uphill. After a difficult day on the bike, I was hoping for a short ride to a campsite. The ride was short, but the vertical climb nearly killed me.

I set up camp, took a shower, and started to settle in for the night. I had no neighbors on either side of me. A few sites down, a family was gathered around a fire in front of their circa-1820 camper. The father yelled down, "Hey, no reason to be by yourself. Come on down." There was a husband and wife, and about a half-dozen assorted grown to semi-grown siblings, step-siblings, half-siblings, and significant others. After settling down by their campfire. I was soon regaled with stories of their adventures. Don't get me wrong—they very were kind, friendly, and generous to me, but they knew the workings of the court systems inside and out. It was like being on an episode of *The Shield*. By the end of the night, I knew which lockups were the best to do time in and which to avoid. I think there was a shiv-making seminar after I left. It didn't strike me then, but they were the first of many socio-ethnic-economic groups that I never would have interacted with if I hadn't taken this trip.

Being in a campground made me lonesome for my family; it didn't feel right to be here without them. In my log that night, I berated myself for being such a wimp. I missed my house and my family. I grieved for a life I knew was gone, baby, gone.

Day Eight; July 2, 2010

Robbinston, Maine, to Machias,

Maine—Forty-Four Miles

The weather was sunny and mild today. The morning was physically hard, but I grew into the day. I almost was starting to feel like a "real" biker. I kept myself well hydrated and ate often and well. US Route 1 in Northern Main is really a country road. Today I was on a stretch that went from nowhere to nowhere. There was no corn, but it did have a definite *Children of the Corn* feel. The road was sparsely populated and indifferently, at best, cared for. Decent-sized cracks filled long stretches of the road. Not just a few here and there—they were everywhere. In places the road looked like a jigsaw puzzle that had been put together by a two-year-old who had eaten half the pieces.

I was able to build up a little karma during the day. I came upon an elderly couple whose car had broken down. They were a little befuddled and in definite need of help. It was very cool to be a bicyclist coming to the aid of people in an automobile. I helped them by calling AAA and giving them directions. It wasn't easy to give them directions; I may have told them they were just past the part of the map where it said, "Here be dragons."

I ended the day in Machias, a mystical place steeped in Native American history—yes, an Alec Baldwin quote from *Friends*. I covered forty-four miles today. I was tired at the end of the day but not totally spent.

Day Nine; July 3, 2010

Machias, Maine, to Milbridge,

Maine—Twenty-Nine Miles

I did a decent day's work on the bike. I didn't cover a great deal of miles, but between the headwinds, hills, and torn-up roads, I felt excellent about my day. The scenery was amazing. It was Maine at its best—classic Northern New England back roads filled with Maine charm. I ended the day in Milbridge, a pretty little town at the mouth of the Narraguagus River. I checked into the Red Barn Inn, a simple but comfortable motel. The lobby even had the quintessential cat sleeping in a basket. After checking in, I walked to a country store for food and fluid for the next day. I was back at the motel for about a half-hour before I realized I had lost my wallet. In a panic I biked back to the store. There my wallet was, waiting for me. The clerk said, "We didn't know where you were, but we figured you'd be back for it."

The Red Barn Inn was a metal-key motel. You know that little plastic key you use to enter your motel room? I've calculated that it costs you forty-five dollars a night. There's an entire class of motel that I call "metal-key motels." These are the motels that in my previous life I would have passed by without even seeing. We were a solid middle-price-motel family. We might if, we had a coupon, step up to a luxury motel. For the most part, however, we stayed in nice—but not too nice—places. On this trip I found an entire lost generation of motels. They were small and family owned and operated. They didn't always accept credit cards. If they did accept cards, I could sometimes get a better deal by paying cash. When I checked in, they handed me a large metal key that would—wonder of wonders—open the door to my room. I found most of these places to be at least equal to chain motels. Sometimes they'd be a little threadbare, but the price was always right.

Day Ten; July 4, 2010

Milbridge, Maine, to Orland,

Maine—Forty-Eight Miles

It was very, very hot today. I felt as if I had taken a wrong turn and was biking on the sun. Sweat dripped off me like a summer thunderstorm. I could see the Powerade coming out of my pores as I drank it. Despite this I made good time and enjoyed myself. The condition of the road was much better; it was almost an actual highway. I biked through classic Maine scenery; it felt like I was biking through a postcard. A good portion of the day I could see Bar Harbor, at first off in the distance then up close and personal. Bar Harbor, Mount Desert Island, is one of the greatest places in the world, with its iconic hiking trails, as well as a series of bike trails built by the Rockefellers, Sand beach, Jordan Pond, the Bubbles and Eagle Lake. It also has one of the best ice cream parlors in North America, CJ Big Dipper in downtown Bar Harbor. If I sound like an ad for Bar Harbor, I am. I spent some of the best times of my life on the Island with my family. It was here where my twins had learned their love of the outdoors. I can still hear them, biking behind me up the Seven Sisters, a fairly challenging uphill climb. They pumped their little nine-year-old hearts, climbing on their Walmart bikes, while their little sister rode in the bike trailer, eating Skittles. I'll admit that biking past Bar Harbor today was more than a little bittersweet. No tears came to my eyes, but it was a close call.

At about 3:00 p.m., I rolled into Ellsworth, Maine, where it was a balmy ninety-one degrees. I rewarded myself with a Frosty at Wendy's. I don't care if there's no ice cream in them; I still love them. I stopped at a bike shop to stock up on Clif Bars and Cytomax. Then I left Ellsworth and pointed my bike south.

As the day cooled off, I felt better and better; I almost felt too good. The darkness of the night caught up with me before I realized it. I don't recommend finding a place to "stealth camp" in the dark. I scrambled around a small Maine village, looking for a place to sleep for the night. Eventually I found a very small park; actually I'd call it a nano-park. Since it was the Fourth of July and I was camping in a public area, I didn't want to draw attention to myself, so I decided not to set up my tent. It was a wonderful night to sleep out in the open, or so I thought. The night was warm, and the sky was clear and filled with a myriad of stars. I even had a peek at the local fireworks. I rolled my sleeping bag on top of my pad and lay down. Soon after I settled in, the assault started. The flying July bloodsucking fiends of Maine had found me. Mosquitos, midges, no-see-ums, and — I swear — a vampire bat descended on me. What kind of an idiot camps in Maine without bug spray? That would be me. I tried to sleep under my tent's rain fly. It worked great to keep the bugs off me, but it was like sleeping in an industrial microwave running on high. I switched to wearing my sweatshirt, sweatpants, and a T-shirt on my head. I looked like a crazy homeless guy who wears all his clothes to bed. I watched the fireworks; it felt very odd to be all by myself on the Fourth of July. I slept fitfully all night. Then I was up at 4:15 a.m. and on the road before five o'clock. I was very excited to be seeing my daughter Shannon in two days.

Day Eleven; July 5, 2010

Orland, Maine, to Belfast, Maine—Eighteen Miles

Being on the road before 5:00 a.m. was a new experience for me; I'm not a morning person. Anyone who has spent time with me can attest to that, but there's something magical about being on my bike early in the morning — just a little bit of a mist, very green grass, and the feeling that the world is empty except for me. I felt transported to Middle-earth again. Around every corner I expected to see Bilbo. Overhead I scanned for Smaug. I would have been only mildly surprised to see the Fellowship duking it out with a band of Orcs around the next turn.

Eleven days on the road was starting to take a toll on my body. My left knee, which is the "good" one, was feeling very sore. For the last several days, I also had an annoying knot behind my right knee that wouldn't go away. I was very glad to have a short ride of eighteen miles today. My legs were really telling me to take a day off. During the trip many people told me to listen to my body; there's a lot of wisdom in that. However, if I really had listened to my body, I would have been in lying in my hotel bed in Fort Kent watching the Red Sox. Yes, you should listen to your body, but sometimes you need to tell it to buck up and do what you command it to do.

I stopped at McDonald's for breakfast—my first-fast food meal of the trip. (I didn't count the Frosty at Wendy's.) I had two Egg McMuffins, which tasted like ambrosia. Loaded with calories and thirty-six grams of protein, they were just what my body needed.

I made it to Belfast early, booked a hotel room for two days, and started to rest. Lately I had been eating ibuprofen like M&M's. It was a dream come true to have an ice machine right near my room; ice on my knee was blissful relief. I took a nap in the afternoon—something else I had taken for granted in my previous life. I slept the sleep of the just. It occurred to me that hotels are a great inventions—and they have TVs! I really enjoyed watching TV and icing my knee and looked forward to doing nothing for forty-eight hours.

Tomorrow I would get to see my daughter, Shannon. This was by far the longest I'd ever gone without seeing one of my girls.

Day Twelve; July 6, 2010

Belfast, Maine

Being in a hotel for two days was a luxury from olden days. Icing my knees for two days was exactly what my body needed. I walked from the hotel to a small Chinese restaurant. I spent the rest of the day resting and trying to contain my excitement as I waited to see Shannon. I felt like a little kid waiting for Christmas morning. I hadn't seen any of my daughters since June 23. By far the worst part of the trip was being away from them. We always had been

23

a very close family. When we were at any sort of gathering — be it weddings or extended-family Thanksgivings — we tended to hang out with one another, so much so that our nickname was "The Pod Family."

The thing I was best at was being a father. If you want to know who I am, spend a day with any of my daughters.

Shannon is an eclectic person with a very stream-of-conscious way of speaking. There's no such thing as a simple answer to a question posed to her. If you were to ask her, "What did you do today?" the answer could very easily begin with, "When I was in kindergarten, I loved playing with blocks." Eventually you'd find out what she had done that day and how playing with blocks was related to it. Sometimes it can be frustrating, especially when all I really want to know is what she had done that day. But if I could be patient, I'd be rewarded with an odd, interesting, and sometimes beautiful story.

Shannon picked me up and took me back to the summer camp — Hidden Valley in Freedom, Maine — where she and her fiancé were working. Hidden Valley is a good match for Shannon. It has all the activities you'd expect at a summer camp, including swimming, hiking, and a ropes course. It also has a wide range of visual art: glass bead-making, bookmaking, painting, and pottery, to name just a few. Its campers come from around the world.

The kids at this camp consider Shannon to be a goddess. Her ability to interact act with these children is truly humbling to me. I think the greatest measure of success as a parent is when your children surpass you. I'm proud to say that I have met that measure.

After a tour of the camp, I had dinner with Shannon and Seann (not a misspelling; that's how he spells his name) at a Thai restaurant in Belfast. This was a real Thai dinner; the place offers great food and its spiciness produces tears of pain/joy. It's true that there's a fine line between pain and pleasure. This was the first time since the trip started that I'd had a sit-down dinner with anyone. This was one more thing on the long list of items that I had taken for granted in my past life.

Shannon dropped me off at my hotel room and headed back to camp. It was hard to see her and Seann leave, especially since today was Nan's birthday. I felt very lonely that night. I still missed her and my past life.

Day Thirteen; July 7, 2010

Belfast, Maine, to Edgemont,

Maine— Fifty -Five Miles

As I was preparing to leave the motel in the morning, the cleaning girls arrived at my room. They were very sweet. When I gave them a five-dollar tip, they were so appreciative that you would have thought they had won the lottery. The economy in Northern Maine was a little more than soft. Over the last two weeks, I had passed closed motels, boarded-up businesses, and abandoned houses. Many of the houses were in the early state of rotting and looked like they could be salvaged. It was very apparent from my bike seat that things were hard here. One of the girls said she was happy if she even found one penny when she cleaned a room. It was exaggeration, but I don't think it was much of one.

Day Fourteen; July 8, 2010

Edgemont, Maine, to Freeport, Maine—Thirty Miles

It was tough to get around Bath and Brunswick. This was the first time that my bike wasn't allowed on Route 1. I stopped at a bike shop in Bath to get directions. They directed me through and around town so I could rejoin Route 1 on the other side of Brunswick. I did a lot of very enjoyable biking, but I didn't make much of a gain on Key West. I picked up a vicious shard of metal in one of my tires after passing through downtown Freeport. I had a very difficult time removing the metal invader. This was my first flat of the trip. I managed to get the tube changed but couldn't get the tire inflated. Luckily I was done for the day.

My niece, Michelle, and her three daughters were coming to visit tomorrow. I was excited and a little nervous. They were not on my side of the family. Michelle is Nan's niece. In my heart

I knew they were still my family, but I still worried. I wasn't sure I could bear any more loss.

Day Fifteen; July 9, 2010

Freeport, Maine, to Saco, Maine—Thirty-One Miles

At 11:00 a.m., Michelle showed up with her twins Liz and Jess and their big sister Renee at the Super 8 in Freeport, where I'd stayed at the night before. They took me to L.L.Bean to get help with my front tire and tube. I never had changed a flat tire before in my life, and when I tried yesterday, it didn't go well. I struggled for an hour—even resorting to using the Internet for instructions— but just couldn't get the job done. It's actually not hard to change a tube out of a tire; later in the trip, I could do it in the dark.

Michelle had me drive. It was bizarre to be behind the wheel of a car. The vehicle felt huge, as if I were at the helm of the *Titanic*. I scanned the horizon for icebergs and German U-boats, then started the beast toward our destination. It felt like we were going at the speed of sound; the car reached speeds of fifty miles an hour. *An hour!* That was a whole day on a bike for me. Automobiles are truly a magical form of conveyance that I had taken for granted.

Once we got to L.L.Bean, I was expecting to pay and arm and a leg, and wait the entire day. The store was very crowded; July is prime tourist season for Maine. The bike shop was full of tourists waiting to get their bikes repaired. The staff exceeded my expectations by far. I learned that the way I'd been treated at Mojo Sports wasn't an aberration. As soon as I told the staff I was biking down the coast, I went to the front of the line, and they treated me like I was a rock star. At the speed of light, my tire was inflated and ready to go, and the price was more than reasonable. They explained what I had done wrong and wished me luck, and we were done.

Michelle took me to lunch at Johnny Rockets, a very cool restaurant chain that re-creates the classic diners of the 1950s. Steel, chrome, and jukeboxes dominate the interior. They do burgers and fries right. I know this sounds like and ad or endorsement, but I assure you I don't have any financial relationship with the chain.

After lunch we went shopping at Abercrombie & Fitch. Yes, you read that correctly—I went shopping with four girls at Abercrombie & Fitch. While I'm biking, I look normal for what I'm doing; wearing a T-shirt and shorts that are covered with a little road grime is the "in" look. At Abercrombie & Fitch, however, I was an anachronism. Pictures of bored girls that are so pretty that it hurts to look at them really contrast with my road-grime chic. At the store I was turning heads with my appearance; look for my new line of clothing in the fall in all the best thrift stores.

After lunch and shopping, Michelle drove me back to the motel. I put my bike back together, and then Renee helped me attach it to my trailer. It was a real treat to have someone to help with this chore; it was a little bit of a pain to do by myself. Then there was the presentation of the gifts. Gifts from loved ones were added to my growing list of things I had taken for granted in my past life. The first gift was a bottle of Sam Adams Summer Ale. I hadn't had a single beer on the trip, and it was a very welcome present. The next was a small metal charm, which I attached to my bike. And last, but not least, was a book about a husband and wife's around-the-world bicycle tour, titled *Far from Home*. The title didn't strike me then. My trip was distance neutral; I was about the same distance from Springfield, Vermont, for most of the trip. My route was following a rough arc of a circle, with Springfield at the center. Geometrical speaking it was a very rough circle. For the next few days, I actually would be moving closer to home—geographically, that is. Metaphorically I was moving away at the speed of thought. I really enjoyed the book; it inspired me. The woman hadn't been a bicyclist before the trip, and I identified with her. Her aches and pains at the beginning of the trip were dead on with what I was going through.

Michelle offered to take me down the road, but I was bound and determined to cover every inch of the trip under my own power. I took some pictures, and then we said goodbye. They drove off at what now felt like a ferocious speed, and I started off at my turtle-versus-hare speed.

In the late afternoon, I hit Portland, Maine. Portland is a great bike town, with lots of bike lanes, an abundance of signs, and courteous drivers. I stopped at a corner hot dog cart that was owned and operated by a young man named Paul. He and one of his customers loved my bike trailer; in fact love of the trailer was a theme of the trip. She was my icebreaker in many situations and perhaps my ticket of credibility. When people saw the trailer, they knew I was a serious biker. Paul very graciously forced a free hot dog on me. Paul's life was a great story. He had walked part of the Appalachian Trail. Then he had poured his last two thousand dollars into his hot dog stand. He'd had the cart for only a few weeks and was just starting to make some money. His customer told stories of how he had traveled the country in his younger days. He talked about sleeping in the woods and tossing rattlesnakes out of his tent. It appears that every cross-country journeyer has a traditional tale of the flinging of the poisonous snake. As a person with a strong herpetological background, I find these stories fascinating, but I suspect many are slightly exaggerated. Every one I've heard is an absolute recipe for how to get bit when interacting with a venomous snake. Both guys were funny and interesting.

Even though Portland is very well marked for bikers, I still managed to get lost—in part by taking a shortcut suggest by Paul's customer. I learned a valuable lesson today. Don't take shortcut advice from a non-biker if you're on a bike. They tend to send you up gigantic hills and on to roads that don't allow bikes. I ended up crossing a bridge on Route 77. Then I found a bike trail that was headed in the general direction I needed to go and that eventually dumped me onto US Route 1.

Day Sixteen; July 10, 2010

Saco, Maine, to Wells, Maine—Twenty-One Miles

The day started great. There was a lot of Maine vacation traffic, but I had enough room to bike. The nice thing about heavy traffic is that the cars go so slowly that there isn't much of a chance of getting hit; in fact, at times today, I was moving faster than the cars. I met a local bicyclist who gave me the heads-up on the road conditions ahead. It was nice to have some company on the road. I passed through Biddeford and then Arundel. As I was leaving

Arundel, the sky opened up, and it started to rain. It came down fast and blindingly — so hard I could barely see. I pulled over and took shelter in the bay of a carwash and watched the rain pour down. For some reason it made me feel very serene; I'm not really sure why.

Coming into Wells I picked up another shard of metal and got my second flat in three days. I was able to change the tube, but again I couldn't get the tube inflated. I rolled my bike to a very nice restaurant, the Bull and Claw. After my recent experience at Walmart, I didn't think I'd get much help. I was hoping they'd give me directions to the nearest bike shop and maybe let me lock the bike behind the restaurant. Much to my amazement, they told me there was no reason to leave it out back. They let me roll it right into the lobby. Walmart wouldn't let me bring my bike in their store, but a posh steakhouse was cool with it. The manager told me there was a bike shop two to three miles down the road.

I took my tire and started walking. I put out my thumb and got a ride almost immediately. A sheet rocker who had just finished his day picked me up. He told me he knew where the shop was and said he would take me to it. He kept saying it was just ahead. We got four towns a way, and there still was no bike shop. Finally he turned to me and said, "I just moved here. I guess I really don't know my way around. Sorry." He dropped me off in York and drove away. It was kind of a crappy thing for him to do. I didn't let it bother me, though. Yes, he was a jerk, but he had to live with himself; I didn't. I started to walk north, back to Wells, where my bike was. A great guy (a real one this time) stopped for me and took me back to Wells. He actually knew were the shop was; it was two miles away from where I had started. This was another great bike shop, Wind and Wave. Maybe all Maine shops are great. They pumped my tire and showed me what I had done wrong. They guy who picked me up waited and drove me back to the restaurant. I hope karma is real; the guy who picked me up the second time deserves to be pulled out of a jam.

My daughter Erin and her boyfriend, and my daughter Jenny and her not-boyfriend, drove from Vermont spend the night with me. They were my first overnight guests of the trip.

ERIN'S STORY

Erin is Shannon's twin and vice versa. They're identical dead ringers. Once a year in middle school and high school, they would switch identities. They went to each other's classes and played the role of the "other sister." They always succeeded. There were only two people in the school who could tell them apart. One was their best friend, Allison, whom they had known since the first day of kindergarten. The other was a boy who had grown into a giant of a man, Casey Lovell; he also had known them since the start of school. To many people Erin and Shannon are identical, and their similarities far outweigh their differences. But there are differences. I can tell them apart by voice, face, and even posture. I love them both for their similarities and their differences. Erin is a scientist. She took her lifelong love of rocks and turned it into a career. Unlike Shannon, she's much more direct when she talks. If you ask Erin for directions, you'll get them turn by turn; you'll have picture-perfect landmarks and arrive at your location. When you get there, you'll find that she directed you to a hidden parking space several feet from your final destination. If you ask Shannon, you may or may not get there on time. You will, however, know where the local Dairy Queen is, and you may drive by the house of a girl she went to summer camp with. Erin is the girl who feels bad about throwing away Popsicle sticks after they've accomplished their purpose. She's the girl who'll hold your hair back when you vomit, even if she doesn't know you. Once, when she was in college, she was walking home with friends after a frat party. One of the girls suddenly collapsed. Security showed up with lights flashing. All the other girls ran, but Erin stayed to help her friend. Erin is deliberate and methodical. She's also kind and empathetic. She's a rare person in this world.

They brought me a late dinner. Best of all, Jenny brought a pie she had baked. She bakes the best pies in the universe. This is a scientific fact that has been proven by NASA. What NASA is doing researching pies is unknown.

CHAPTER THREE

The Rest of New England

Day Seventeen; July 11, 2010
Saco, Maine, to Danvers,
Massachusetts—Fifty-Seven Miles

I started the day with breakfast in Ogunquit, Maine, at the Egg and I. My company stayed and shared breakfast with me. This was another first for the trip — a family breakfast. It was very nice to have such great company in the morning. I don't remember our parting being sad. I think I had been so happy to see them that it overshadowed any feeling of sadness. It would be a long time before I would see any of my girls again.

JENNY'S STORY

Jenny was the youngest (and baring expensive surgery) the last of my children. Nan and I were very gun-shy about having another child after the twins. After we'd had Shannon and Erin, we'd met a woman at church who'd had twins a few years before us. She and her husband had decided they wanted to have a singleton. She got pregnant nine months after their twins were born. Nine months later—you guessed it—they had a second set of twins. She told us, with a mixture of laughter and tears, what it was like to have four children under eighteen months of age in diapers. Sometimes she'd just lie on the floor and cry as they crawled over her. We also worried what a singleton's life would be like with twin siblings. The twins were so popular; we couldn't go anywhere without the populace wanting to be around them. People would stop us all the time to tell us how cute they were. Everyone had a story about their twins—or said that they were supposed to have twins or that their second cousin twice removed had twins. In short everyone was enthralled with Shannon and Erin. What would life be like for their younger brother or sister? Would the child always be in the shadows? Would he or she always be the younger sibling of the incredible twins? Would the child become a drug-addicted, Amway-selling serial killer? We were so concerned that we almost didn't have another child. That would have been a terrible tragedy—a tragedy for us, the twins, and the world at large.

We took the plunge and had a third child. Jenny was born in 1992, and the world was a much better place immediately. Jen was born with beautiful, extremely red hair. She was the end cap to our family. All of our concerns about her being lost in the twins' vortex were soon put to rest. Everyone who saw Jen wanted to talk to us. They wanted to tell us how cute she was. Everyone had a story about how they were redheaded or said that their sister was redheaded or their second cousin was redheaded.

Jen was mature before her years but not in a distrubing way. She wasn't the kid you wanted to punch because she was a know-it-all narcissist. She was the kid you wanted to hang out with because she was cool, calm, collected, and compassionate. She wasn't the kid who sat at the cool kids' table; she had no need for that. She was cool without even knowing it.

As the fellowship of Vermont set off to return to their mystical homeland, I headed south on Route 1. I hoped today would be my last day in Maine. As much as I loved Maine, seventeen days is a long time to bike through one state.

If you've persisted in reading this far, you're probably wondering, *Why is he still in Maine?* Isn't this book about a trip from Maine to Florida to San Diego? Where are the other states? The simple answer is that Maine is a big state. In New England most of the states are small; Rhode Island can fit in a Hello Kitty backpack. Maine is the exception that proves the rule (which is a moronic saying). Maine is a huge state. On top of that, I didn't take the most direct route through the state. I biked about 525 miles in Maine. To put that in perspective, it wasn't until I was in Maryland that I had more miles out of Maine than in it. The entire trip from Fort Kent, Maine, to Key West, Florida, was 2,570 miles; 20 percent of the trip was in Maine. Yes, Virginia, there is a State of Maine, and it's a big-ass state.

I had made it to Kittery when I had a problem with the trailer. As I was fixing it, the rain started to pour. Tlaloc, the Aztec god of rain (and fertility, but that ship already had sailed) kept a very close eye on me. If he saw that I had my bag open and exposed, he'd dump rain on me unmercifully. I had some luck, however; Tlaloc must have had more pressing business, as it turned out to be just a short thunder shower. It was over in a few minutes. I jerry-rigged a fix, which I knew wouldn't hold too long, and headed to the bridge into Portsmouth, New Hampshire. I stopped for directions to the nearest bike shop and made my way there. The bike techs at Papa Wheelies improved on my jerry-rigging but didn't have the parts needed to put the trailer back into mint condition. I was sure it would hold, at least for a few days. The price was outrageous — free. After biking seventeen days through Maine, it took me a leisurely afternoon to get through New Hampshire. That included the bike repair and lunch. I spent the night in Danvers, Massachusetts; I covered 56.8 miles today and a total of 555 miles so far.

Day Eighteen; July 12, 2010
Danvers, Massachusetts, to Dedham,
Massachusetts—31.5 Miles

I got up this morning very excited to attempt my first urban biking experience. Boston was on today's agenda. I love the city of Boston. I have been a Celtics fan since conception and have become a diehard Red Sox fan. Being in Boston was great; I felt like I was on home soil for the first time on the trip. I was a little leery, however, of biking through the heart of the city. Anyone who ever has driven through Boston can testify that there's no quarter given or taken by Boston drivers. Most of them consider driving to be a full-contact sport. Red lights are a guideline. To be obeyed or not obeyed at the whim of individual drivers. I also was pushing my luck, because I hit the city at the start of rush hour. I was very surprised at how Boston drivers reacted to me on the road. I could see the road rage building in them as they jockeyed for position, looking for any weakness in their opponents. When they saw me, however, they'd stop their urban games of metallic jousting and wave at me. Then they graciously made sure I could pass. It was surreal.

I biked through Somerville and into Cambridge. In Cambridge I stopped at a bike shop where I got excellent directions. The excellent directions, however, didn't stop me from going the wrong way on Mass Ave. You may have had the advantage this time, but we will meet again. That is my promise to you, Mass Ave. — we will meet again. The mistake wasn't a complete disaster, though; I got to see the towns west of Boston. I ended up near Dedham, where I took a side road parallel to Route 1. On the road I met a local bicyclist named Peter Raymond who gave me a mini bike tour of Dedham. He took me past a very quiet, unassuming building where Sacco and Vanzetti's trial took place. I found it fascinating that such an important, violent event in history was housed in what is now a picturesque and idyllic setting. I covered 31.5 miles today; tomorrow I would end my short time in Massachusetts. I'd be across the border in Providence, Rhode Island, staying in my first warm-shower accommodations.

Day Nineteen; July 13, 2010

Dedham, Massachusetts, to Providence Rhode, Island—Thirty-Five Miles

I took Route 1A from Dedham to Plainville, Massachusetts; it was a lovely ride through tree-covered Attleboro. About eighty years ago—at least that's what it felt like—I used to live here. I was living there when I started dating Nan. I shared the upstairs apartment with the owner of the building; it was in a pretty rough locale. When people were coming to visit, the last step in the directions were "Go past the fire-bombed building. We're two houses down." I slept on a two-inch foam pad in a room with no curtains. The foam pad was on loan from a friend. After this start, I should be happy that Nan stayed with me for twenty-five years, not twenty-five minutes.

I crossed into Rhode Island around 3:00 p.m., took pictures and videos of the welcome sign, and had an ice cream. After being in Maine, I felt like I was flying through states. I stopped at a package store and bought beer as a present for the people I was staying with. The manager of the store was fascinated with my trip. He followed me out to examine my bike and trailer. He also helped me strap the beer to the trailer. The beer gave the trailer a severe case of lopsidedness. Weeble-like, but not falling down, I made my way down the residential streets of Providence. I looked like a homeless alcoholic who was transporting his day's supply to his van down by the river, where he was living with the ghost of Chris Farley.

I was staying with people I had connected with through warmshowers.org. The site is flat out one of coolest things in the world. It's a community of people who open their homes to bikers who are on tour. The website lists places to stay on every continent except Antarctica.

With great directions from my host Amelia, I found the house without any trouble, but the trailer was giving me a hard time again. One of the bushings that attached the trailer to the rear axle was missing. I had managed to jerry-rig it so the trailer would stay on, but it had gotten to the point where the trailer would stay attached only if I was going more or less straight. Unfortunately I would have to make at least one left turn to get to Key West. It started to pour just as I reached the house; luckily I arrived before I was completely drenched. Amelia and her housemate Sarah were very gracious. I was afraid it would be weird staying with complete strangers, but it wasn't; in fact it was one of many unexpected cool things I experienced on this trip. We split a Cajun chicken pizza and drank a few beers. I had four beers, a record for the trip; they went right to my head. I slept safe and sound on Amelia's air mattress — warm, dry, and a little buzzed.

Day Twenty; July 14, 2010

Providence, Rhode Island, to Stonington,

Connecticut—Sixty-Two Miles

The first stop this morning was Legend Bicycle in Providence. They did a great job of putting the trailer back into shape. They replaced the missing parts and made a few adjustments to the bike while I watched the Tour de France on TV. As usual I got great service and a head-of-the-line pass. I wasn't sure I deserved it, but I was getting VIP treatment at every bike shop went to.

As I rode out of Providence around noon, the temperature was in the low eighties, and the humidity was very high. Despite the humidity, it wasn't a bad day to ride. A light rain cooled me off every hour or so, but the heat made it very hard for me to eat. Staying hydrated was much easier; I did a good job of keeping fluid on board. Near the end of the day, my muscles started to beg for food. In fact they all but forced me to stop. I had the best $3.50 hamburger ever at the Hitching Post Restaurant. My extreme hunger may have had something do to with it, but I would highly recommend the Hitching Post in Charlestown, Rhode Island, to any biker.

I was discovering that Route 1 was a very unpredictable mistress. One moment she was a divided highway with traffic roaring by, and then, in a heartbeat, she became a sedate country road — a road littered with beautiful horse farms, riverside views (swains included), and mom-and-pop restaurants. I crossed into Connecticut quietly, with no marker to let me know I had entered. Connecticut was the last of the New England states I would bicycle through. Ironically the only New England state not included was my home state of Vermont. I covered sixty-two miles today, a new personal record for the trip and for myself.

Day Twenty-One; July 15, 2010

Stonington, Connecticut, to New Haven, Connecticut—64.7 Miles

My first stop today was for pizza in Mystic, Connecticut, but not at Mystic Pizza. The locals steered me away from there. I ended up dining at Pizzetta. Filled with my favorite bicycling food, I started toward New Haven, my goal for the day. The miles had been easy yesterday; today they came at a steep price. Every mile seemed to stretch out to the horizon. I felt likeI was on a Connecticut-size treadmill. I should have known I was in for trouble when the road out of Mystic was called Rod Serling Road, next stop ahead Twilight Zone, Connecticut. After biking forever I saw a sign that read, NEW HAVEN — 32 MILES. I biked another twelve miles and came to the next sign, which read, NEW HAVEN — 32 MILES. Then, after another twelve miles, I spotted a sign that read, NEW HAVEN — 30 MILES. Was I going in circles? Was I traveling on a New England Möbius strip?

The next sign read, NEW HAVEN — 30 MILES. *Ed, give up,* I thought. I may have hallucinated the last sign. When I finally made it to New Haven, the sun was setting. One of the challenges of being on a bike is finding your way across water. In some places there's a bike path beside the highway, other times not so much. Getting across the river led me through some interesting parts of New Haven. I went through a Hispanic neighborhood at about 8:30 p.m. It was very colorful and vibrant; Spanish signs where everywhere, and Spanish poured out of every bar. The area had a reputation for being rough, but I felt entirely safe. I heard a lot of comments from the street, ranging from "Nice bike" to multiple questions regarding whether the bike was for sale.

I arrived at Carissa's building at about eight forty-five. It was great to see her. I had met her when she was four. Her father, Gerry, had been my supervisor at Springfield Hospital. He, his wife Judy (no, this is not a *Jetsons* riff), his son Joe, Carissa, and their baby sister Jenny had come to our house in Enfield, New Hampshire, for a visit. It was Christmastime, and they had come to see the holiday lights at LaSalette Shrine. The lights at LaSalette are a big deal. They're set on a hill in a life-size setup of the Stations of the Cross. We walked around the lights, oohing and aahing, while the kids got to know one another. At the end of the night, as Gerry and Judy put Carissa into the car, she burst into tears. She looked at my twins as if they were her long-lost sisters and cried, "I'll miss you guys." I can still see her teary-eyed face as they drove off.

Now, eighteen years later, I was rolling my bike into her apartment. She recently had graduated from nursing school. It was good to see her joining the world of grown-ups with a great job, a nice apartment, and a good life. We went to a bar/restaurant on a corner near her building for a beer and something to eat. It was a little odd to have beer with her — not as odd as it was with the twins, but darn close. She had a great couch that felt like a small piece of heaven.

Today I set a new personal record of 64.7 miles, for a total of approximately 750 miles. Tomorrow I'd rest then set off again the following day.

CHAPTER FOUR

The Lands of My Youth: New York, New Jersey, and Pennsylvania

Day Twenty-Three; July 17, 2010
New Haven, Connecticut, to Rye,
New York—Fifty Miles

After spending an entire day resting at Carissa's, I left New Haven feeling refreshed. It was still very hot outside; the highest temperature I saw was ninety-seven. I had a late breakfast of pizza at the Pie Hole in Orange, Connecticut, and saved room for dessert, a milkshake at Dairy Queen. It was the height of hedonism. I saw my first—and, as it turned out, only—lemonade stand, of the trip in Fairfield, Connecticut. Two little entrepreneurs, Olivia and Hazel, had set up shop in a upscale commercial district. They were competing with vintage clothing stores, luxury candy shops, and five-star restaurants. They appeared to be very sharp businesswomen. They were holding their own in the dog-eat-dog world of street-corner lemonade sales. They gave me the choice of pink or regular, for twenty-five cents a cup. I splurged and had two of each. They were by far my favorite street vendors of the trip. Later I stopped at a produce stand in Westport. They were making smoothies with a blender out of ice and fresh fruit. I felt like I'd had a shot of adrenalin after I gulped down my drink.

I crossed into New York today. This was a watershed moment for me. Until this point I hadn't been moving away from home. I had more or less been the same distance from Springfield, Vermont, for the first part of the trip. My house—well, my old house—felt like it was the center of a big circle. I had been biking attached to an emotional tether on the circumference of that circle. While I was in New England, I could, in an almost physical sense, feel the pull of that attachment. It was both a comfort and burden. I didn't want my old life to be over, and as long as I was still in New England, I could fool myself. I was still a short car ride from my house, my couch, my daughters, my TV, and my soon-to-be ex-wife—a woman I was still in love with. I could fantasize that this was just a vacation, a short break from the familiar, an emotional respite.

I knew once I crossed into New York the journey would turn south. I realized the tether would have to stretch and then break. I knew this to be true and that it had to happen. All of this knowing, however, didn't keep me from not wanting it to happen. It didn't stop me from being brokenhearted. I didn't want to turn south; I wanted to point my bike north and head home, but that wasn't possible. My home no longer existed. It was just a well-loved memory.

I made it to Rye, New York, by nightfall. I checked into a hotel so I could watch TV for the night. I didn't want to think anymore.

Day Twenty-Four; July 18, 2010

Rye, New York, to Jersey City,

New Jersey—Thirty-One Miles

I approached New York City on a Sunday morning. The traffic before I hit the city was remarkably light. In some of the places, the streets were all but void of people. I saw a ton of storefront churches. It appeared that each one had its own outdoor loudspeaker. This led to what I coined "The Doppler Word of God." I was regaled with each sermon as I passed. The sermons started out low in volume, then increased until I was in front of the church, then faded away. As one sermon faded away, I'd start to hear the next one. This—combined with the dearth of people—gave the start of the day a very apocalyptic feel.

Riding into and through New York City turned out to be a blast. Getting through the city was slow going, with lots and lots of traffic and red lights. Stopping at the all the street vendors cost me the most time. I felt like a goat in a tin-can factory—so much to eat and so little time. The New York drivers were very tolerant of bikers; there were a ton of "us" everywhere. When I got to the George Washington Bridge, I had some trouble finding the entrance to the bike path to cross into New Jersey. After a little searching, I eventually was able to find the path. Crossing the George Washington on the path was an experience unto itself, with wide lanes and breathtaking views of the city; I was in awe. The roads on the other side, in Northern New Jersey, were a nightmare to figure out on a bike. They were a can of worms—nightmare worms with fangs dripping venom. I poked around the worm nest of death, looking for a road that didn't lead to instant death. The drivers that had been so tolerant in New York had transformed into road warriors that had survived the zombie apocalypse. They were the Nazgûl of drivers, ready to feast on your flesh then pick their teeth with your bones.

I ended up following the Hudson down the coast of New Jersey to free myself of the tangle of roads that marked the end of New York and the beginning of New Jersey. The Manhattan skyline was appropriately impressive from the New Jersey side. I passed through Hoboken, which is famous for being Frank Sinatra's hometown. I finished up the day in Jersey City, where I stayed in a Ramada in a Middle-Eastern neighborhood. I wandered around looking for an ethnic dinner, which I found in plenty. After wandering into a Middle-Eastern convenience store/deli, I came upon another unexpected joy of the trip—foods I never had eaten before, some of which I never had heard of. The man behind the deli counter had a look of slight confusion as I tried to order. It was very obvious that he wasn't used to having an English-speaking customer. I didn't feel any ill will, more like wry amusement. Between pointing and pantomime, I was able to get something that I'm pretty sure had beef in it. Whatever it was, it was both strange and delicious. I retired to my room after my feast, content and relaxed. I had covered thirty-one eventful and exciting miles today. Tomorrow night I would stay with my niece and her fiancé in Southern Jersey; it would be great to be with family.

Day Twenty-Five; July 19, 2010
Hoboken, New Jersey, to Pemberton,
New Jersey—Seventy-One Miles

The laws that govern bicycle riding In New Jersey are some of the most favorable for bicyclists in any of the states I traveled through. It was apparent, however, that the drivers of North Jersey hadn't gotten the memo or just didn't care. It was a hard day's ride, to say the least. I spent most of the day on US Route 1/9. New Jersey drivers are brutal. No physical debris was actually hurled at me, but it wasn't church bells I was hearing all day. I believe New Jersey truckers get paid a fee based on the number of times they frighten bikers with their horn.

It was very hot and humid during the first part of the day; the air had a liquid feel to it. It was almost like breathing maple syrup. The heat off the payment was extremely intense. You couldn't have cooked an egg on the road, but you could have heated up your lunch. I left Route 1 and took 130/206/38 to my niece's house. This was my first real departure from Route 1 that wasn't predicated on the route being closed to bike traffic. It was a little hard to leave her; I had come to think of the route as a physical being. She was a little moody. Sometimes she was quiet, calm, and serene (as she was in most of Maine); other times bustling, busy, and awesomely beautiful (New York); sometimes exotic and strange (the Hispanic neighborhoods of New Haven, Connecticut); and sometimes a little dangerous and unpredictable (Northern Jersey). She had become my companion on the trip, my second rider, and I would miss her.

42

The traffic was still heavy for most of the day. At one point a driver rolled down his window and told me, "Hey, this is Jersey—that's dangerous." With a little swagger, I shrugged and said, "Life will kill you" (a quote from Warren Zevon, one of my favorite musicians). This was one of the few times in my life that I had acquired "cool" status. I've gone back to relive in that moment many times.

As I biked down 206, the weather turned very *Wizard of Oz*. The sun was setting, but it was still completely visible above the horizon. The clouds were very weird colors and shapes. Ahead of me, to the south, I saw very dark storm clouds brewing, and a strong wind was blowing in my face. I started to look for a tornado funnel. Suddenly there was a short burst of hail and a scattering of rain; it was nothing serious, but I was concerned that it could be a harbinger of severe weather.

In the middle of this, I came across traffic backed up very far for construction. I felt that secret joy I'm sure all bikers feel as I sped by traffic in the breakdown lane. Being immune to traffic is one of the secret superpowers bikers have. It might not have made me Spider-Man, but it felt damn close.

I came to the road-construction flag man and discovered another superpower. Flag men look at bicycles very differently than cars. If they think it's safe, they just wave you through. They realize you can slide safely through most of the construction. After passing the flag man, I had the road to myself. I pedaled right down the middle of the lane, with construction workers waving me on.

It was starting to get dark. As I got close to my niece's house, there was a light on-and-off rain. I had another discovery—Southern Jersey drivers were much nicer than drivers in Northern New Jersey. One truck driver pulled over and asked me if I needed a ride. I was taken aback after being locked in near mortal combat with the drivers all day. I thanked him and let him know that I was almost "home."

A few minutes later, as I stood on the side of the road checking my Google map on my trusty iPad, a car pulled over to make sure I was OK. I know I've maligned and harangued New Jersey, but the residents of South Jersey made up for their Northern counterparts.

I pulled into Katie's neighborhood around eight that night. She was pushing her daughter Haley in her stroller while they waited for me. I can't describe how wonderful it was to see Katie. She had been the flower girl at my wedding at the tender age of two-and-a-half. We had been warned that she was far too young to pull off the duties, but she had done it without a hitch. Two years after my bike tour, Haley would be a part of the flower-girl contingency at my daughter Shannon's wedding.

Katie made me a grilled cheese sandwich, a huge comfort food to me. Then she made a second one for me. Then, just to make sure I didn't die of malnutrition, she made a third. These sandwiches have gone down in the annals of grilled cheese as the best ever. They've received the coveted status of "legendary" by the International Grilled Cheese Sandwich Association. While I was eating these, Haley's job was to keep me hydrated. Apparently the automatic water dispenser on the fridge is normally off limits to her, but she was allowed special dispensation during my stay to use it to keep my water glass full. She took this assignment very seriously. As I ate, she stared at me and the glass of water. If I wavered in drinking it, she'd very firmly yell, "Drink it!" I felt like I was at a bizarre spring-break drinking contest moderated by a three-year-old. Her firm insistence that I drink my water soon had me well hydrated and in stitches.

I biked a record seventy-one miles today.

Day Twenty-Six; July 20, 2010

Pemberton, New Jersey—Rest Day

I slept the sleep of the dead. After waking up at eleven thirty, I spent a relaxing day with Katie, Haley, Doug (Kate's fiancé), and Doug's dad, Ed. Doug cooked steaks on the grill; I'd had two home-cooked meals in less than twenty-four hours. I was living the life of kings of yore. Staying with family for two days filled my heart with joy.

Day Twenty-Seven; July 21, 2010

Pemberton, New Jersey, to Abington,
Pennsylvania—Thirty-Three Miles

Today I had a very short day planned. I was headed to Abington, Pennsylvania, to stay with the father (Phil) and stepmother (Ann) of a nurse I had worked with at Springfield Hospital. Meredith was one of my favorite nurses (to be fair, my list of favorite nurses is very long). She's an eclectic person — razor thin, with a razor wit to match. At the time she and her husband lived in a rustic one-bedroom cabin on a farm owned by her mother and stepfather. The farm was located on a long dirt road at the end of a steep hill. I had visited once, during the winter of my separation from Nan. During my visit I was driving my van and got stuck halfway up the hill in the snow. I made a quick call to Meredith, and she was on the way to my rescue. I so wish I had a picture of her coming down the hill. Dressed in her farmer's clothes and driving an old tractor, she looked like the quintessential Norman Rockwell farm girl. She hitched up my van and pulled me out of the bank. I parked the van at the bottom of the hill and rode the tractor with her up the hill. There's something very magical about riding on a tractor deep in the Vermont woods on a crisp winter night. The light of the moon reflecting off the tree boughs covered with snow and ice had a quiet, breathtaking beauty. The stillness of the night, contrasted with the steady, calm, comforting sound of the tractor chugging up the hill, was exhilarating. The dinner I had with her, her mother, and stepfather was succoring. I brought beer, as any good guest should — Yuengling Black & Tan, which was met with the appropriate oohing and aahing. I spent a very comfortable night there, filled with good conversation, food, and of course beer.

I took it very easy today; I ate an early lunch at Hooters, for the first time. I must say I really enjoyed it. The food was surprisingly good and the waitress very nice. Afterward I thread my way through some lovely residential neighborhoods, then crossed into Pennsylvania on the Tacony-Palmyra Bridge. I had a lazy ride through the northern suburbs of Philadelphia. A few houses down from my destination, I met a woman and her three-year-old son. The son was very excited about my bike and all my gear. He picked up my folding yellow sleeping pad and just took off, at the speed of child, trailing it behind him like it was Superman's cape. His mother was apologetic and very embarrassed, but all I could do was laugh.

I wasn't sure what to expect from Phil and Ann. I knew they were Quakers, but my only knowledge of Quakers was from my high school history classes, which happened a long time ago in a galaxy far, far away. When I rode up to the house, Phil was sitting on the front porch, waiting for me. I knew everything would be OK when he said, "If I gave you a beer, would you know what to do with it?" He brought me a Yuengling; I guess good taste in beer is hereditary.

While we were sitting on the porch, drinking beer and talking like old friends, a census worker made her way up to us. She was doing follow-up work and was looking for a non-existent address. She sat and talked with us for a while. During the course of the conversation, she told me I would be considered homeless by the census bureau. I found this interesting; I suddenly realized I was homeless, but at that moment, it really didn't bother me. In fact for a long time I wore the title as a badge of pride.

Ann showed up shortly after that. A little while later, Phil cooked hamburgers on the grill. Three days of home cooking in a row? Three days in a real home, sleeping in a real bed? I just hoped I wasn't getting soft. It was very cool to see a framed, hand-drawn card placed proudly on the wall that Meredith had made. Phil and Ann were great hosts. We spent a few hours conversing about my trip, the state of world, and whatever came up. I was surprised at how at home they made me feel. It was heartening to stay with such great people again. I went to bed feeling fat and happy.

Day Twenty-Eight; July 22, 2010
Abington, Pennsylvania, to Kennett Square,
Pennsylvania—47.7 Miles

I started the day with a bowl of Cheerios with Phil. He had been working on a route for me through Philadelphia. He sheepishly told me he was sure I'd already had the best route mapped out. I didn't and had pretty much planned on winging it with my iPad and luck. Later that day I would find out that the route he had laid out was a thing of beauty. It took me on a peaceful and beautiful bike trail. I could hardly believe I was in the middle of Philadelphia. I could still hear traffic, but it felt very far away. The trail reminded me of the carriage trails in Acadia National Park in Maine. There was a wonderful little restaurant in the middle of the trail system, a sort of mini Jordan Pond house. I spoke with a bunch of bikers, adults and kids. I was more than a little sad when I had to leave the park and return to "real" roads.

Once I was out of the park, the heat of the day hit me full force. I rejoined my girl, US Route 1. I didn't know if she had missed me, but I had missed her. Traffic was heavy as I left Philly.

After almost a month, eight states, and closing in on a thousand mile, I had my first real run-in with an angry, arrogant, ignorant driver. A van driver opened his door and yelled at me that I was ridiculous and that I should get off the road. When I told him he should read the laws regarding bicycling, he resorted to a very effective method of refuting my point of view—he unleashed a torrent of obscenities. The funny thing was that traffic was moving so slowly that for the most part I was going at the same speed as traffic. I also had been passed by multiple police officers who'd had no problems with me. I rode Route 1 until it was closed off to bicyclists. I had to route myself through a mall parking lot and then take secondary roads; the roads were scenic and great to ride on, until I reached Rose Tree Hill. It started out vertical then got worse. I'm sure Lance Armstrong did the Tour de France instead of doing this hill. Mountain goats took cabs rather than climb this hill. I finally managed to get back to Route

1 but was pretty much busted for the day. That night I stayed in Kennett Square, the mushroom capital of the world. They produce over a million pounds of mushrooms a week. According to www.historickennettsquare.com, 51 % of the nation's mushrooms are grown in Southern Chester County, P.

I biked 47.7 miles today, but with the side trip up Rose Hill, it felt like 47,000.

CHAPTER FIVE

Maryland, Virginia, and North Carolina

Day Twenty-Nine; July 23, 2010
Kennett Square, Pennsylvania, to Cockeysville,
Maryland—Sixty-Five Miles

There was a change in the temperature today. Instead of being very hot, it was organ-destroying hot. At one point I'm pretty sure my spleen melted. The temperatures were only in the mid-nineties, but the heat index had skyrocketed to 105 then 115. I've lived in the Northeast all my life. I've always known that the wind-chill factor was a real thing, to be ignored at the risk of frostbite and amputation of fingers, toes, and noses. But I'd always thought the heat index was just a thing to fill up the bottom scroll on the Weather Channel. I now realize, beyond any doubt, that it's very real. The ninety-degree temperatures in Maine now seem like a distant Arctic dream.

Despite the heat, I was making good progress on US Route 1—slow and steady but consistent progress. The road had a great shoulder, with a ton of room for my bike. A short burst of a police siren behind me changed all that. The state trooper told me the road was limited access, and bicycles weren't allowed. When I asked him if I had missed a sign, he said no; it was just understood. The laws in Pennsylvania are a bit vague. In some places on the exact same roads the police would just wave. This officer was very professional. He didn't give me a ticket; he just asked me to get off at the next exit.

On secondary roads conditions were harder and more dangerous. Route 1 had been straight as an arrow. It had hills, but they were long, with very little slope. The secondary roads I was on now were a nightmare in comparison. They were winding, with multiple lefts and rights. The hills were steep and took their toll on me with gleeful joy. The worst thing was that the shoulders were just a rumor. Plus this was no quiet country road; traffic was heavy. My goal was to get to the Conowingo Bridge Motel, about thirty miles away. This would give me a reasonable ride to my friends' Rich and Eileen's house in Glyndon, Maryland, where I was staying the next day. I crossed into Maryland at about the one-thousand-mile mark of the ride. I distinctly remember looking down at my legs at that point. They were covered with scabs and bruises (I was always bumping into something). They were tan and had muscle definition that I hadn't seen since I was eighteen. I was totally amazed that they had carried me a thousand miles; it just didn't seem possible.

I also crossed the Mason-Dixon Line today; I took the obligatory picture and moved on. When I got to the Conowingo Bridge, I saw that the motel was long gone. Nothing but a shell remained. My map had let me down badly. Spending the night in the tent had no appeal. The weather was still demonically hot, and I craved a shower and A/C. I would have settled for a campground shower, but even that was not to be. I stopped at the next general store to ask if there were any motels or campgrounds in the area. They just shook their heads and told me there were some near Baltimore, which was forty-plus miles away. I decided to just keep riding toward Rich and Eileen's and hope for the best.

The dark caught up to me in a hurry. I don't mind biking at night. I have a strong headlight and find the moon and stars to be a real comfort. The only real worry I have is being hit by a car. I do have plenty of rear lights, but they only go so far in protecting you at night. The roads I ended up on were true rural Maryland roads—convoluted, narrow, and with no shoulder. The cars passing all seemed to see me, as they all slowed down, but it was wearing on my nerves. I pulled into Cockeysville at pitch dark o'clock. Sitting outside a convenience store, chugging Gatorade, I stared forlornly at the lights of a Comfort Inn. They beckoned and tempted me. They whispered, "Come and spend the night with me. It's only money." It was just ten miles to Rich and Eileen's, but it was too far. Finally I surrendered. Feeling weak and a little pathetic, I walked my bike across the street and got a room for the night.

In retrospect it was the only sane solution. The heat of the day had driven me to near exhaustion. I was fighting dehydration and hunger. On top of that, the roads were too narrow and dark to traverse at night. Still there was a stubborn part of me, deep in the reptilian part of my brain, that wanted to go on. Staying the night there turned out to be an excellent decision. After I lay down on the bed, I realized the rough shape my body was in. Everything hurt. I was having cramps in places where I didn't know I had muscles. My toes battled with one another to see which could do the best imitation of a Russian contortionist. The judges are still out on who won. If I had gone to the local ER, they would have wanted to start an IV to replace my electrolytes. Sleep eluded me until 2:20 a.m.

My total miles today were a respectable sixty-five.

Day Thirty; July 24, 2010

Cockeysville, Maryland, to Glyndon, Maryland—More Miles than I Thought

Sleeping late at the hotel seemed like a good idea; checkout was at noon. It had been a rough night, and the rest was blissful. Rich and Eileen's house was a mere ten miles away in Glyndon,

Maryland. I could do that riding backward on a unicycle. In my mind this would be a cake walk. My mind, however, was way off base; it wasn't even in the stadium. Staying late at the hotel proved to be a monster-size mistake. The temperature was in the low one hundreds, and the heat index was 120 by the time the rubber hit the road. After the first few miles, I felt like I was biking through an Easy Bake Oven. The sun felt like it was three inches from my head. The heat and humidity were beyond belief. The heat of yesterday was a nostalgic memory — ah, if only the heat index were 105! That would be heaven. I rested every mile or two at the most.

The country I passed through was gorgeous; majestic horse farms dominated the landscape, one of which belonged to Cal Ripken, Jr. The miles were painfully slow, almost as if time had come to a standstill. The next to last road I was looking for was Butler Road. When I saw it, I was so relieved; the day was almost done. The road started with a moderate climb. At the top of the hill, I stopped at a beautiful Episcopal church, Saint John's. My iPad told me it was three miles to their house. It felt like I had biked much more than seven miles, but it was hot, and I was sure my judgment was a little off. I cruised the next three miles downhill to the end of the road. Ah — just another half-mile, and I'd be there. I stopped at a little general store to gets some fluids. I was so glad to be done for the day; I had almost nothing left in me. I spoke to the girl behind the counter. I was a little confused; the roads didn't seem to match up with my map. I asked her where Glyndon was. She said, "Not far. Just go up that road, and turn right." She pointed toward the road I had just come down. A horrible sinking feeling came over me. I did another search on my iPad. I was now 6.9 miles from my destination. I looked at the map and realized that where I had taken a right on Butler Road, the road also went straight. At that turn I almost could have seen their house. I had gone 6.5 miles in the wrong direction. That moment may have been the worst of the trip. I didn't think I could go another mile, let alone another 6.5; and the last half of Butler Road had been downhill. I didn't cry, but I did consider self-mutilation.

I got my breath and started back up Butler Road. I pedaled, pushed, and almost crawled back up the hill. The sweat pouring into my eyes was so concentrated that it felt like hydrochloric acid. I was stopping at increments of less than mile. Twice I had to lie down for fifteen minutes to rest. I stopped again at St. John's Church; my clothes were so covered in sweat that it looked like I had been sprayed with a hose. I finally made it to Rich and Eileen's neighborhood — two hours later than I expected and biking more than twice the miles.

Rich and Eileen were away for the weekend and wouldn't be home until the next day. The house was so cool that it was like I had walked into heaven; I love A/C. I sat with my back to the front door. Alfred, their dog, barked at me for five minutes. They had warned me that he would bark until I gave him a treat. Once I had sat down, though, I just couldn't get back up, not even to give Alfred the treat he was barking so hard for.

After five minutes I managed to get over to the dog treats. As soon as Alfred had his treat, I was his best friend in the world. He followed me around the rest of the day. That night, as I slept on the couch, he used my clothing bag as his bed.

Days Thirty-One and Thirty-Two; July 25–26, 2010

Glyndon, Maryland—Rest Days

Alfred woke me to be fed and walked. I spent the rest of the day being lazy, watching TV, writing, and napping. I never will take napping for granted for the rest of my life. Rich, Eileen, and their kids showed up around 5:00 p.m. I'm truly thankful to have friends like them. I hadn't seen them in years, yet they took me into their home as if it had been only days since we had last seen each other. Eating with a family was wonderful and filled me with a warm feeling. It was bittersweet to be sure. I missed my family, but it was great to feel like a small part of a family, even for a few days. A second night of sleeping in the same place — with the knowledge that I would be getting a third — was very comforting.

Rich had to fly away for business the next day. Eileen was nice enough to drive me around town so I could stock up on supplies,

Clif Bars, electrolyte powder, and bananas. The night was topped off with another home-cooked meal.

Day Thirty-Three; July 27, 2010
Glyndon, Maryland, to Arlington,
Virginia—Sixty-Five Miles

It was hard to leave. I didn't get on the road until close to noon. Eileen took a picture of me biking away. I was sad to leave such good friends, but I also was excited to get on the road. The day was so much cooler than the last few days had been. It was still hot, but the heat was compatible with life. My destination today was Arlington, Virginia, to stay with another friend of the twins, Alison Bromell.

It was a great day of riding. US Route 1 took me right through the heart of West Baltimore. I had been advised not to bike in this part of town—something along the lines of "They kill people there." West Baltimore is dirt poor, and the buildings that were in use were rundown. Those that were abandoned had rotting wood, broken windows, and graffiti everywhere. During most of the ride, I was the only white person around. I never heard anyone say a cross word or even give me a dirty look. A small group of children swarmed around me at one point. The trailer and the bright yellow bag, as usual, were a magnet for kids.

While I was talking with some children, four men rolled up on me. This was the closest I had come to being in a tense situation during my time in West Baltimore. They were making sure I wasn't a danger to the kids. Once they saw I wasn't, they were full of questions about the trip, the trailer, and the bike. When I told them I was headed for Key West, one little boy, who was about eight, asked me, "Why don't you just hitch a ride?" I wasn't sure how to answer that, so I just said I wanted to ride there.

There was a bustling economy going on in the streets. People's shops were folding tables set up on the sidewalk. I stopped at one of them that sold food and drink. They had about a hundred flavors of snow cones. The flavors ranged from the mundane orange and grape, to the slightly odd Mountain Storm, to the truly bizarre

Wine Cooler (no particular type, just Wine Cooler). Burgers and hot dogs were cooking on the grill. No health-inspection certificates, no nutrition information, and no gaily dressed employees were in sight. There was also a brisk business going on out of the building behind them — single beers for sale. Capitalism was thriving in its purest form in the ghetto of Baltimore. Everything was priced at a dollar, except for the water bottles, which were fifty cents each.

I had an orange snow cone and spent some time talking to the man running the store and his eighteen-year-old female helper. They were fascinated — and I think a little bewildered — by my trip. It was obvious they were well acquainted with depression and its effects on people. After finishing up my treat, I decided to buy a couple of bottles of water. I didn't really need them, but these people had been kind and were genuinely interested in me and what I was doing. The young woman working there told me I couldn't buy anything else at the store. She opened a well-worn change purse and pulled out a dollar in change and dropped it in the till. Her simple gesture humbled me. It was clear that she had next to nothing but was willing to share what little she had. I still think of her; an eighteen-year-old angel raised in poverty had taught me a life lesson in generosity. She was one of many angels who touched me on the trip.

Between Baltimore and D.C., I had my second bad encounter with an angry driver. In sight of a SHARE THE ROAD sign, a morbidly obese woman driving an expensive SUV told me to "get the F out of the road." I did manage to keep my cool and thank her for the advice, which incensed her even more. Ironically, not five minutes before, another woman had told me how cute my trailer was. The stark contrast between this woman and my angel of the ghetto made me laugh and cry at the same time.

At dusk I entered D.C., hot and tired. I stopped at a Rita's for custard and a cool drink; it was very refreshing. Bicycling through D.C. was a breeze, even in the dark. The streets were so well lit that it felt like it was still day. Traffic was heavy with both automobiles and bicycles. I did regret that I hadn't planned any time to explore D.C. by bicycle. I made it to Alison's in

Arlington at about 10:00 p.m. I had covered sixty-five miles on a thought-provoking day.

Day Thirty-Four; July 28, 2010

Arlington, Virginia, to Dumfries, Virginia—28.9 Miles

Today was hot and humid right from the start. It took quite a while for me to wander out of Arlington. At one point I almost stumbled onto Interstate 395 by accident. I finally got to US Route 1, which is also known as the Jefferson Davis Highway. There was a ton of traffic. Stop-and-go traffic is a pain in the neck on a bicycle, as well as a car. In Alexandria I went past a tiny restaurant, Blue & White Carry Out. I thought it was closed; the building looked like it was at the point of collapse. I rode by, hoping I'd find another place to eat soon. Two feet past it, the smell hit me; in fact it spun me around like a top. I leaned my bike against the outside of the building and walked into one of the culinary wonders of the world. Inside there was a small area were you ordered. It was so narrow that two people could barely pass each other. The area where they were cooking had just enough room for three people, but somehow four people were whizzing around at breakneck speed. The paint was peeling, the ceiling was crooked, and there was no A/C, but the smell of the food was intoxicating. My saliva glands cramped in anticipation of my meal. One of the cooks handed me a paper menu. I ordered the chicken breast sandwich for $3.30. He told me for that price I got two sides; I picked mash potatoes with gravy and corn. When the meal came, I had a chicken breast, a drumstick, potatoes, corn, and two pieces of bread. I ate at the side counter (room for one), with sweat pouring off me as I had one of the best meals of the trip. People started coming in left and right, ordering food, telling the cooks which piece of chicken they wanted, how much hot sauce, and extra gravy or less gravy. It was a gastronomical ballet. I left feeling like I'd had one of the great food experiences of my life.

The rest of the day was physically hard on the bike. The heat, humidity, and maybe the chicken had taken its toll on me. I had heavy legs all day and called it quits in Dumfries, Virginia.

Day Thirty-Five; July 29, 2010
Dumfries, Virginia, to Tappahannock,
Virginia—Seventy-Five Miles

When I was at Rich and Eileen's, we had looked at giant map that graced their mud room. After some discussion and thought, I decided to leave Route 1 and take 17 to the Outer Banks. For years the Outer Banks had been on my list of places I'd wanted to visit. Today my plan was to get to Fredericksburg and take 17 southeast to the Outer Banks.

The day started like yesterday, very hot and humid. I feared I wouldn't be able to cover many miles today. My stomach was nauseous almost from the start of the day. Stomach issues had been a part of my old life; they had plagued me to no end for years. On the trip, however, they hadn't been an issue. I was more than a little worried that my old physical ailments were catching up to me.

Hot and tired, I struggled to get to Fredericksburg, which is a very neat town. It's definitely on the list of places where I would like to spend more time. I stopped at a little smoothie shop to cool off and get some fluids. Feeling refreshed after some A/C and a vitamin-packed smoothie, I got back on the road. As I pedaled out of town, the temperature took a sharp, welcome drop; the weather forecast included thunderstorms. I turned left on Route 17 shortly after leaving Fredericksburg. The road became much more of a country road than I was used to over the last few weeks. This was also a welcome change. I heard and saw evidence of a thunderstorm all around me, but nothing hit me directly. My day had turned around. At the start of the day, I'd felt like crap, but now I was feeling great. With the lower temperature, and for the most part a good shoulder, I felt like I could bike forever. I kept biking until dark then biked some more. As I came into Tappahannock, Virginia, it started to pour, so I decided to look for a room for the night. I pulled into the Dollar Inn, which felt like a weird omen ("Dollar" had been my college nickname). I covered seventy-five miles today and felt fantastic.

Day Thirty-Six; July 30, 2010

Tappahannock, Virginia, to Gloucester Point, Virginia—Fifty Miles

I decided to actually plan where I would stop for the night. This was the first time I'd done this on the trip, unless I was staying with someone. I chose Gloucester Point, about fifty miles from Tappahannock. I looked online and found a campground. It was really relaxing to have my destination picked. It was unbelievable to me that I could bike fifty miles and have it feel like a rest day. The campground had a very tribal feel. Most of the sites were permanent, with trailers (long houses) that had golf karts (horses) parked outside. Everyone seemed to know one another, and people rode from trailer to trailer to visit as the night went on. My site was beside a pond, just a few yards from a small tidal river. It was very comfortable and familiar to hear the frogs calling all night long. The stars were stunning, and the night sky was clear. It was still hard for me to be in a campground at night. I found myself thinking that I had to get the campfire going for the night. I expected to hear the girls playing outside, to see Nan getting dinner ready. I just missed everyone so much at night in a campground.

I got an unexpected phone call when I was tucked into the tent for the night. Rich called to check on me; it was nice to hear a familiar voice. It helped make the loneliness a little more bearable. I slept solidly and had no back or hip pain in the morning.

Day Thirty-Seven; July 31, 2010

Gloucester Point, Virginia, to Chesapeake, Virginia—Fifty Miles

I left the left campground at around 11:00 a.m. I think I may be the latest-starting bicyclist in the history of touring. I headed south again. When I got to Newport News, Virginia, I crossed the James River Bridge. The bridge is a lift, which I hated biking over. The bridge started out with a little hill. When I arrived at the top, I got a bit worried. The bridge went on forever, and there was no shoulder. Later I found out the bridge is four-and-a-half miles long. Traffic flew by me at sixty-plus miles an hour, inches away from turning me into an Ed-shaped stain on the road. I was toughing it out and thinking there was no way a bike should be allowed on the bridge. At the three-quarter mark, I found out I was right. A state worker in a flatbed pulled around me and stopped in front of the bike. He told me that bikes weren't allowed on the bridge. He made me put my bike on his truck and transported me the rest of the way. These were the first miles that my Surly and I didn't do on our own. He pointed out the signs that clearly stated that the bridge was off limits to bikers. At the end of the bridge, a Virginia state trooper was waiting for us. He reiterated that I didn't belong on the bridge. I think my borderline groveling and apologetic manner saved me from being tasered and ticketed.

I spent the rest of the day weaving in and out of the towns of Portsmouth, Stratford, and Chesapeake. I went through a very rough part of Chesapeake. Everyone seemed so angry. I thought I was going to see a knife fight in a convenience store over change. A young man made a small purchase and threw his money at the clerk. The clerk made change and threw it back on the counter. The customer, his voice starting to rise, said, "My change should be ninety cents." The clerk, his voice also rising, said, "How much does it look like?" The customer nearly shouted, "Ninety cents. Oh, so I'm the bad guy?" The anger was palatable. This was first place on the trip where I'd been afraid. No one threatened me or did anything overtly antagonist toward me, but it felt like I was in a bizarro Hallmark movie, *The Town that Forgot How to Smile*.

Day Thirty-Seven; August 1, 2010

Chesapeake, Virginia, to Jarvisburg,

North Carolina—65.1 Miles

This was a terrific day to bike. The weather was much cooler and partly cloudy when I started for the day. I didn't get far before I saw a bake sale for a girls' soccer team. I stopped and bought some cookies and talked with the girls and their parents for a while. Then I followed Route 17 toward North Carolina; the road was beautiful, with full shoulders. I biked along the Dismal Swamp Canal toward the Dismal Swamp, a big state park in North Carolina. I kept expecting to see Saltheart Foamfollower — five thousand bonus points to anyone who knows who that is. The road passed through cornfield after cornfield; there's a boatload of corn in North Carolina.

When I entered North Carolina, the shoulder all but disappeared, and the speed limit went up. It turned out to be all right, though. Almost all of the drivers gave me plenty of room. I stopped at the first rest area, where I picked up a North Carolina map and a bike map for the Outer Banks. I was able to find a bike trail that paralleled Route 17. I eventually got onto Route 345, off the bike trail. It's a very nice country road; it felt great to be back in the land of no traffic. A light rain kept me cool but not soaking wet. On Route 345 I spotted a small bear abandoned in the middle of the road. He looked sad and forlorn. I couldn't just leave him there, so I picked him and strapped him to my handlebars. No, he didn't bite me. He was a tiny stuffed bear, missing one eye. I carried him for more than a thousand miles; then one day he was just gone. I like to think he's living a great life in the wild, or in the bedroom of a five-year-old red-haired girl.

I came into the small town of Camden, North Carolina, at the junction of 345 and 158. In the parking lot of a small country store, in the back of an old pickup, was a group of kids. They were dancing, waving signs, and selling spot. I stopped to ask them what a spot was. It turned out it's a fish. A couple of more kids came running out of the store; suddenly I was the afternoon entertainment in small-town North Carolina. I spent the next half-hour going over the trip with them in detail; I never got tired talking about the trip. After I left my fans in Camden, I pedaled down the road to Jarvisburg. I was standing outside the Frog Leg Seafood Market, checking my iPad for directions. While I stood there, a thunderstorm struck, and rain came down like canines and felines. I went into the market to get out of the rain and to get something warm to eat. I had cream of crab soup, which was warm and delicious. I ended up meeting most of the staff, who were very interested in the trip. I spent a lot of time talking to them and various other people in the market. It was still raining when I left—it was heavy but rideable, I thought. I was completely soaked in seconds, but at least the rain wasn't cold. The rain stopped a few minutes later, and I was able to get in a few more miles. I stopped at the Sea Oats Motel; it was too wet for me to face setting up the tent in the wet and dark.

Day Thirty-Nine; August 2, 2010

Jarvisburg, North Carolina, to Kitty Hawk,

North Carolina—Thirteen Miles

I took a short day and did some sightseeing in Kitty Hawk. I hadn't done much real sightseeing on the trip and wanted to spend some time in the Outer Banks. It was a quick thirteen-mile ride from the Sea Oats Motel to the Wright Memorial Bridge. The Wright brothers seem to be kind of a big deal here. The south side of the bridge had a very narrow shoulder. It was as small as the one on the James River Bridge that I had been removed from in Virginia. The difference was the drivers. They gave me a lot more room and traveled at a much lower velocity.

That night in Kitty Hawk, I camped at Adventure Bound Campground, which is attached to a small hostel. The hostel had only a few rooms left. At one point, during the golden era of hostels, it had been a major complex with dozens of rooms. The owner clearly missed those days. Due to changing economic times, he had been forced to convert most of the rooms into apartments. He had gone from being a freewheeling member of the counter-culture to an established landlord. The campground still retains some of its 1960s-'70s feel. The sites had no numbers. You got to set up where you wanted and move tables as you pleased—a small taste of anarchy. I set up my tent in a small wooded area. Then I detached my trailer from my bike, stored my bag, and set off to explore Kitty Hawk.

It felt strange to bike without the trailer, and keeping my balance was a challenge for a few miles. Once I got my balance straightened out, I was biking at an almost alarming rate of speed.

After having pulled the trailer for the better part of five weeks, I had forgotten that I could go fast on a bike. I was the Flash, zipping around the Outer Banks.

The Outer Banks were everything I'd hoped they would be—beautiful beaches, a serene sound, and today a calm, cooling ocean breeze. Everyone should mark it down as a place to visit. I did take a weird, hard fall, however. I came to a stop sign as I biked toward the ocean. My tire went off the road and onto the sand shoulder. The sand turned my tire ninety degrees and brought the bike to a sudden stop. I toppled off the bike in slow but painful motion and hit the asphalt hard. In the process I gave myself a hip bruise and a strained neck; they became more war wounds that I wore proudly. That evening I stopped at a local pub and treated myself to prime rib and two beers. I spent a restful night in my tent; two beers had sent me off to a quick sleep.

Day Forty; August 3, 2010

Kitty Hawk, North Carolina, to Avon,

North Carolina—Fifty-Four Miles

Another hot day—what else? I followed the Dare County bike route, which took me on bike trails, through residential side streets, and by the ocean. As I biked past a restaurant, I noticed two bikes loaded for tour parked outside. I stopped and found a couple, who were a little older than me, having breakfast. They had come from England with their bikes to tour the East Coast. They had started in Savannah, Georgia and were headed for New York. The husband had biked all over the world, including a trans-America trip. It was a real treat to meet and talk with other people on tour. The wife was very taken with orange Gatorade; she sounded like it had saved her life and sanity on the trip. It was an international day, as our waitress was from Slovenia. Later that day I would meet a family from Taiwan when I took their picture on Pea Island.

I spent a good part of the day at Pea Island Wildlife Refuge. The refuge is approximately thirteen miles long (north to south) and ranges from a quarter-mile to one mile wide (from east to west). I loved having the ocean on one side of me and the sound on the other. I stopped at the rangers' station to listen to a talk about wildlife in the area. There I spoke with a family who turned out to be from Western New York, near where I had gone to high school and college. The husband had gone to college with a set of twins from my high school whose father was an old basketball buddy of mine!

Bicycling the Outer Banks is a blast. Flat, scenic, bike-friendly roads made this part of the trip a joy. There was one major draw-back, though — there was very little shade. The sun was relent-less, with very little chance to escape it. Eventually I spotted a road sign that provided enough shade for me to lie down for a few moments. I rolled out my sleeping pad and enjoyed a short respite from the sun. Little did I know that the island's wildlife was attacking me, stealthily and ruthlessly, as I innocently rested. A hoard of chiggers was attempting to turn me into a mobile buffet.

After my short break, I biked into Avon. I had a flat tire and limped into a campground, where I secured the last site. The campsite next to mine was occupied by two young, cute Canadian girls. Listening to them speak in French was familiar and strange at the same time.

I was showering at the campground when I noticed that my legs, just above my ankles, were covered in ugly, raised welts. Several of them were bleeding. At the time I thought it was a rash or contact dermatitis from something I had come into con-tact with that day.

Day Forty-One; August 3, 2010

Avon, North Carolina, to Ocracoke Island,

North Carolina

The next morning I hobbled into Island Cycles, where I picked up a couple of new tubes for my tires. I told one of the clerks about my welts, which were still very painful and red. He told me immediately what they were — chigger bites.

Warning: The following includes graphic descriptions of the effects of chigger bites and may not be appropriate for small children, the squeamish, or arachnophobes. Chiggers are the juvenile form of certain mites. Mites are arachnids. That puts them in the same class as spiders and ticks. If you're still reading, good, you're not a wimp. In the Outer Banks, they lie in wait in vegetation for unsuspecting hosts. They're just barely visible (1/150 of an inch) to the human eye. The actual bite is painless, but it causes a hardening of the skin in the area called a stylostome, a tube from which they can feed. After they bite they inject potent enzymes that cause the tissue to liquefy, creating a cellular smoothie. They then suck this up—I assume with arachnid relish. The injection of the enzymes causes painful itching and—for me—oozing welts on the skin. Like many juveniles, they aren't overly bright. Humans aren't appropriate hosts for them. They're brushed off easily and don't burrow under the skin. Their delicate mouth parts are destroyed in the process. This kicks them out of the evolutionary game. The fact that the little miscreants had died to cause me pain was little comfort.

That night I stayed at the Beachcomber Campground. It really was more of a people corral than a campground. It was a bare, circular piece of land, surrounded by a fence, with no-fuss campsites. I didn't think we were being held for slaughter, but... It wasn't my favorite campground of the trip, but it did the trick for the night. I walked around Ocracoke, had a beer at an outdoor bar, and called it a night.

Day Forty-Two; August 4, 2010

Ocracoke Island, North Carolina, to Morehead City, North Carolina— Sixty-Three Miles

A terrific storm woke me in the middle of the night. It shook the tent like the Big Bad Wolf. I attempted to videotape the storm, but all the video contained was darkness and my hoarse voice. The storm passed without transporting me to Oz, so I drifted back to sleep. I woke early up to catch the ferry. I had left most of my clothes out during the storm, a poor man's laundry. I threw everything into my bag and got ready to leave. My back tire was flat again; the patches just wouldn't hold. I pumped it up as best I could and rode the couple of miles to the ferry. The ferry cost three dollars for a bike—what a deal. I had planned on changing my flat on the ferry, but it was so windy that everything was in danger of blowing off the ship. I decided against it and just enjoyed the ride. The ferry ride was about two-and-a-half hours long. It dropped me off at Cedar Island, where I changed out the tube from my rear tire and was good to go.

This was the first day that I'd biked in regular shorts, not the padded shorts I'd purchased for the trip. This was one of my worst ideas of the trip. My nether regions were very unhappy and let me know very loudly at the end of the day. The road out of Cedar Island was as flat as Kansas and ran through a wildlife refuge. There were no houses and very little traffic. It made me feel like I was the only person in the world. The road seemed to stretch out in front of me forever. There was nothing but light poles to mark my passing, and a very strong headwind slowed me down. I climbed a steep bridge as I pulled into Morehead City. After I crested the top of the bridge and started downhill, the wind was so strong that it felt like it would hold me in place if I stopped pedaling. I saw a flashing sign for a hotel that served waffles for breakfast. That clinched it for me; I needed a place to dry out all my stuff, and waffles in the a.m. would be ambrosia.

Day Forty-Three; August 5, 2010

Morehead City, North Carolina, to Burgaw,

North Carolina—Eighty Miles

I woke up early and decided to try to get to my niece and nephew's house in Burgaw, which was about eighty miles away. I put my head down and biked hard. I came through Jacksonville, a military town. Every five feet I passed a barbershop. Being a barber must be a great business when everyone gets their hair cut twice a day. After leaving Jacksonville, I saw another biker on tour going north. He yelled, "Where are you headed?" I yelled, "Key West. How about you?" He yelled, "Maine." We stopped and talked; he had started in Charlestown, South Carolina, and was traveling very light. It was amazing to me how little gear he had—not much more than a bivy sack, the clothes on his back, and a water bottle. He was tearing up the road, though, doing close to a hundred miles a day. I was very impressed and more than a little jealous about how fast he could travel. He said he had been doing mostly stealth camping.

My nephew Bradley, his brother Joel, Joel's wife Jessica, and Joel and Jessica's daughter Lauren live together in Burgaw, North Carolina, a small town fifteen miles outside of Wilmington. They're an exceptional family. They have a well-balanced, slightly out-of-the-norm, well-run household. Jessica was nine months pregnant; I arrived on her due date. She was a great hostess. Despite being due to deliver at any second, she had been in regular contact with me. She wanted to make sure they had all my favorite foods and, more important, beer ready for my arrival. For years Bradley and Joel had lived together. They had proclaimed themselves, jokingly, heterosexual life partners. When Jess entered Joel's life, the three of them decided to live together. They've done an amazing job of balancing the lives of three adults and now two children.

I pulled up to the house around 8:00 p.m.; Bradley was in the driveway filming my triumphant arrival. It was so wonderful to see them. Lauren was a little shy at first, but she warmed up very fast. They had dinner waiting, which was great. Their goal during my stay was to put all the weight back on me that I had lost during the trip. The Red Sox were playing the Yankees. This was a perfect storm for my stay. The boys are huge Yankee fans, and I'm a diehard Boston fan. Not much could be better than watching the Sox hammer the Yankees while having the boys bring me beers and getting constant attention from Lauren. She's a beautiful blond little girl, and her ability to roughhouse is almost unsurpassed. I was posted at the end of the couch; she would fly down the couch and launch herself into the air, her elbows flying and knees aimed at my head. Then she'd make solid contact with me. She made a serious attempt to knock me out every time. It was like being in a WWF SmackDown, toddler edition.

After throwing down a few Fat Tires, I stumbled upstairs to the futon that had been reserved for me. I went to sleep very content.

Days Forty-Four to Fifty-Three; August 6–14, 2010

First Intermission

My time with Teriburys was very important to my well-being. The physical rest was key to my body's recovery. The mental rest was equally important. To be with people I loved, who were just happy to see me, was restorative to my spirit. Being there was like drinking from a secret fountain of healing.

While I was there, I was able to reflect. I thought a lot about my depression. The trip had taught me several things so far. I could no longer think of myself as lazy. I had biked too long and hard to believe that. The idea of laziness no longer had credibility. Knowing I wasn't lazy was a major relief to me.

The power of exercise also had become an indisputable fact. The more I exercised, the better I felt. I could no longer deny the effectiveness of being outside. The sun, the wind, and the rain on my skin all made me feel alive and happy. Even the pain associated with being on the bike was life affirming. The journey — the traveling from point A to B — was healing me.

Mental pain was still with me every day, but it no longer defined me.

The rest of my time at the Terribury household was a blur. I spent a great nine days with Bradley and Joel, Jess, Lauren, and the new baby, Ryan. They treated me like a king, waited on me, and stuffed me with food and beer; it was one of the best times of my life. It was very hard to say goodbye.

Day Fifty-Four; August 15, 2010

Burgaw, North Carolina, to Shallot,

North Carolina—Sixty-Eight Miles

The Teriburys fed me one last great meal. I hugged everyone goodbye and was on my way. It was such a gift to be able to spend so much time with them. The first day on the bike was fantastic. Being back on the road was like coming home. My legs felt terrific; I think the days off made them stronger. The temperatures were in the high eighties, which didn't feel bad at all. I biked through Wilmington to Carolina Beach. Then I biked along the coast, passing through Carolina Beach and Kure Beach. I took the Fort Fisher ferry from Kure Beach to Southport. Everything was going well. My legs felt strong; my stamina was top notch; and my spirits were high. Then out of nowhere I had a wave of nausea. What caused it was a mystery. I was keeping up my fluid intake, and the heat didn't feel onerous. I think my body was just used to being fed too much food and beer. I still managed to get in just short of sixty-eight miles.

CHAPTER SIX

South Carolina and Georgia

Day Fifty-Five; August 16, 2010
Shallot, North Carolina, to Myrtle Beach, South
Carolina—Twenty-Seven Miles

Last night was rough. I couldn't get to sleep until 3:00 a.m. I had muscle cramps. They weren't as bad as they were early in the trip, but they were worse than they'd been in a long time. I was up and out early in the morning. The temperatures weren't bad — in the mid-eighties. The first hour went great. I crossed into South Carolina early in the day. Fireworks were available immediately; the first fireworks store was within inches of the border. After I crossed into South Carolina, the temperature jumped to the mid-nineties. The shoulder completely disappeared. The drivers weren't bad, but there wasn't a lot of room. I also had a lot of trouble with sweat in my eyes; I stopped often to rest and rehydrate. At one point I took a bad tumble. I came off the bike, almost over the handlebars. I bruised my hip; I also bruised my ego, as I had an audience.

The heat and humidity pounded me relentlessly. I guzzled fluids as fast as I could, but it still wasn't enough. I was slathered in sweat and South Carolina dust. I was covering the miles but paying a steep price. I looked like a man who had walked out of the Sahara Desert. Suddenly I saw an oasis ahead—a Hooters. Covered in road grime, dehydrated, and close to exhaustion, I leaned my bike and myself against the wall of the restaurant. I must have looked near death. A couple of waitresses came outside. Scantily dressed, beautiful, young waitresses—they were a shimmering mirage. I was weak and wobbly, but a smile still came to my face. If I were going to die on the road, being surrounded by Hooters girls would be a good way to go. They escorted me inside, to the blessed relief of air conditioning. Gently they guided me to a booth, brought me water, and oohed and aahed over me. My introduction to Myrtle Beach was a rousing success. After being rejuvenated at Hooters, I returned to the road. I managed a few more miles and stopped for the night.

Days Fifty-Six to Fifty-Seven; August 17–18, 2010

Myrtle Beach, South Carolina, to Huntington Beach,

South Carolina—Twenty-Seven Miles

I made it a very short day. The heat was brutal; I wasn't sure if it worse than before or if I hadn't re-acclimated to it. I was drinking fluids as fast as I could, but I couldn't keep up. After a short ride, I arrived at Huntington Beach State Park campground. To get to the campground, you have to cross a waterway that has one of my favorite signs, DON'T FEED THE ALLIGATORS. I wondered if I'd have to pay a fine if one chowed down on me. I got a campsite for two days then quickly biked to the site to take a nap. I rolled out my sleeping pad under a shade tree and lay down. I didn't set up my tent or unpack any gear; I was too tired. I fell asleep in a heartbeat and woke up a few hours later. The sun had set, and the darkness disoriented me. I was starving and ordered a pizza to my campsite. I was surprised that the pizzeria was completely nonplused by the order. It was a first for me, but apparently they did it all the time. I ate my pizza, showered, and went to bed.

As usual I was careful to make sure I didn't leave any food out. That didn't stop a troop of juvenile raccoons from paying me a visit. Despite my scolding them, they examined every piece of equipment I had. I was worried that I should have locked up my bike; I'm pretty sure one of them tried to take it for a spin. His legs were too short to reach the pedals, though, and he gave up. The raccoons finally left after I threatened to leave the tent. Later one brave soul returned and tried to get in the "back door" of the tent to try to get the last slice of pizza I was saving for breakfast. That was a mistake — you can take my life, but you can never take my pizza. My *Braveheart* screams sent him fleeing.

The next day I rested. I know a lot of bikers see the sights when they take rest days, but I rest. Whatever was going on with me was hanging on; my fatigue wouldn't abate. I slept early and often. Just as the sun was setting, I went to the bathroom to take a shower. When I returned I discovered the raccoon gang had raided my camp while was gone. I could have sworn that I had zipped up my tent, but the flap was open. They had opened a small box of Clif Bars and taken the bars. Then they had carefully and neatly torn off one corner of each package and eaten the bars. It was a very neat and clean operation. They did everything but leave a note.

Day Fifty-Nine; August 19, 2010

Huntington Beach, South Carolina, to Georgetown, South Carolina—Approximately Fourteen Miles

Hoping to start early and beat the heat, I got up at 4:00 a.m. I made sure my camp was secure before leaving it to the mercy of the Huntington Beach raccoon gang and headed to the shower. I left the campground as the sun was rising. The bird life surprised me as I crossed the causeway to leave the campground. Birds of almost every size and color were at the water. I was in awe and felt I was in for a great day — but that was not to be. Within minutes of getting on Route 17, I was exhausted. My legs felt like they each weighed a ton, and I was breathing like a fish out of water. I found myself stopping after less than thirty minutes to rest. I lay on my sleeping mat and caught myself just before falling asleep. I realized I need to find a place to get out of the sun for the day. I managed to bike a few more miles and crossed the bridge into Georgetown, South Carolina, at about 9:30 a.m.

I had struggled all morning and managed less than fourteen miles for the day. I felt dejected. How could I be so weak? Was I too feeble to accomplish this trip? This was the low point of my journey; I felt helpless and hapless. I was at the point of tears when I pulled into the parking lot of the Quality Inn. If they couldn't give me a room, I probably would have collapsed into a hot mess right there. The woman at the front desk took one look at me and realized I needed help; she did everything but carry me to my room. The relief of being out of the heat and in a cool, dark room overwhelmed me, but I also felt ashamed for being such a weakling and also felt a touch of fear. What if this was it? If the trip ended here, it would be a major failure for me. At this point in my life, a failure might literally kill me. I stripped down and briefly thought about getting in the shower, but instead I turned on the TV and crawled into bed. TNT was airing a rerun of *Supernatural*, one of my all-time favorite shows, but I didn't even make it through the opening theme song. I was out in a flash — as if I had been run over by a train. I woke before the sun set, feeling great. I was able to wash my clothes, which were way past due for a good cleaning. I went to bed and slept soundly through the night.

Day Sixty; August 20, 2010

Georgetown, South Carolina, to Charleston, South Carolina—66.1 Miles

Today was much better. I felt very good early in the day, although I was a little leery that it wouldn't last. I stopped at a roadside produce stand for a break. I bought a bag of grapes and sat inside the stand while I ate them. The man running the stand had skin that was black as coal and looked ancient and wise. He had a quiet dignity that made him seem even wiser. I felt like I was in the presence of someone who had the answers to life. We spoke for a while, but I couldn't find the question that would unlock the mysteries of the universe. I left feeling—well, I don't really know. Maybe I thought I was on the brink of having a breakthrough, of understanding something important. Or maybe it was just the heat.

A little while later, I stopped at a small diner and had a great burger with a side of lima beans. I had forgotten how much I love lima beans. They must have something I was low on because I felt completely energized after eating them. While I was eating, there was a major thunderstorm, with lightning and thunder like it was the end of the world. The rain stopped while I was eating. When I left the restaurant, it returned but was slow and steady. I reached Charleston around 4:30 p.m. I biked along the Arthur Ravenel Jr. Bridge, which crosses the Cooper River. This was one of my favorite bridges of the trip. It's a cable-stayed bridge, which reminded me of the Bunker Hill Memorial Bridge in Boston. The bridge in to Charleston offers one major improvement—a bike lane separated from traffic. It was a joy to ride on.

Day Sixty-One; August 21, 2010

Charleston, South Carolina, to Yemassee,

South Carolina—Fifty-Seven Miles

The day started off hot—eighty-seven degrees, with a heat index of ninety-seven. For the second time on the trip, I got caught short, and this time it wasn't on some lonely road. I had to hightail it behind a closed dialysis unit to take care of business. The grapes from yesterday had caught up with me.

Biking had become fun again. After the wall I had hit, it was a gigantic relief. My mental state was soaring. I stopped into a country store that was filled with obscure flavors of jams, salsa, and barbecue sauces. It was like being in a Vermont country store. I bought a small piece of pound cake and a soda. I ate and sat in a rocking chair as I watched the world go by. A thunderstorm hit while I was undercover, and then a motorcycle pulled up. The rider got off and came to speak with me. He said he had seen me up the road. He laughed and said he thought I was making better time than he was.

I waited it out for about half-an-hour. During a lull I made a run (bike) for it. Suddenly it started to pour, and I was soaked to the skin in seconds. There wasn't much I could do but keep pedaling. I was aiming for Yemassee, South Carolina, where I knew there was a cluster of motels. I was planning on getting out of the wet for the night. The rain was on and off, but it stayed with me for the rest of the day. The rainclouds made it get dark early. When I got to Yemassee, I picked a Knights Inn, which cost a whopping twenty-nine dollars for the night.

It's good advice not to drive your car through water that covers the road; that advice counts doubly for bicycles. As I pulled into the hotel driveway, I started to ride through a puddle. Just as my front tire went into the puddle, I realized the water was about two feet deep. Somehow I managed to hop/jump off the bike and land on my feet, just like Spider-Man. Amazingly neither my bike nor I suffered any damage. I checked into my room and started my well practiced ritual—the drying of the clothes.

Day Sixty-Two; August 22, 2010

Yemassee, South Carolina, to Savannah,

Georgia—Forty-Five Miles

Despite the heat I was able to keep up with my fluids and food. I took a detour off Route 17 then followed Route 25 through Alligator Alley. I just couldn't pass up a trip through Alligator Alley. I felt a little cheated, though, as I didn't spot gators anywhere. I crossed quietly into Georgia, with no sign or marker. The plant life took a fairly dramatic turn once I crossed into Georgia. The Spanish moss hung thick from the trees, giving the area a gothic feel. I soon fell in love with the back roads of Georgia. Pecan plantations sprung up all around me. For the most part, state lines are fairly arbitrary; however, I felt like I'd been transported to another land when I crossed into Georgia. The heat was still riding shotgun with me, but I had more shade to protect me. The heat that had been killing me was only wounding me now.

I didn't feel like Superman, but I was feeling stronger. I was now out of the grip of whatever Kryptonite had been sapping my strength in South Carolina. The world was looking much better, and the end of the trip seemed a fait accompli. As I wound my way through the back roads of Georgia, I saw the road sign that bikers fear most, BRIDGE OUT — DETOUR. A detour when you're in an automobile can be annoying. When you're on a bicycle, it can be life changing. I stopped at a convenience store to rest. Looking at my map, I was allayed; the detour would take me less than a mile out of the way.

I arrived at the Springhill Suites in the middle of Savannah's historic district. The room, which was courtesy of my friends Rich and Eileen from Maryland, was too nice and big for me. It had a sitting room (in case I was planning on entertaining), a giant flat-screen TV, and a shower large enough to play badminton in. I had arrived early enough to take a shower and explore Savannah. The city was filled with music, as multiple outdoor concerts were taking place. Many of the bars featured live music also. I stopped at a pub and ordered a beer. When they asked me if I wanted it in a to-go cup, I was shocked; the only other places I knew where you could get beer to go were New Orleans and Key West.

I met a very nice couple at the bar. They were going on a ghost walk and invited me to go with them. They even offered to pay for my ticket. People's generosity continued to amaze me. I turned down their offer, however. I was tired and wanted to get on the road early, with a clear head in the morning. Savannah very much reminded me of New Orleans but without the overt sexuality. On the way back to the hotel, I saw a man riding around on a bicycle. I was about to call out to him when I realized he was screaming obscenities at the top of his lungs. I hoped he wasn't a glimpse into my future.

Day Sixty-Three; August 23, 2010

Savannah, Georgia, to Darien,

Georgia—Approximately Sixty Miles

Temperatures were high again; the heat index reached 102, but there was plenty of shade covering the road. I kept a slow and steady pace today; I rested often and kept my fluids up. The worst thing about today was the beating the boys took. My bicycling shorts had just about given up the ghost; they'd been in the dryer one too many times. The "codpiece" had melted and was misshapen, and no longer did the job of protecting my "guys."

I saw my first armadillo (dead) today. I covered just over sixty miles, making this my fourth consecutive day of fifty or more miles.

Day Sixty-Four; August 24, 2010

Darien, Georgia, to Woodbine, Georgia—Forty Miles

It was still hot today; the high temperature was eighty-nine, with a heat index of 101. The roads, however, offered plenty of shade, which made it fairly comfortable for biking. I saw a ton of dead armadillos on the road; it was like I was passing through Armadillo Armageddon (Armadillagon?).

One of the reasons so many armadillos meet their demise on the road is because of their defense mechanism. When an armadillo is startled, it jumps into the air. This can cause a predator to be startled and allow the armadillo to escape. Automobiles almost never fall for this. The jumping reflex also causes them to jump into the undercarriage of cars, while other animals use the cowering method survive.

I covered forty miles today. My legs were a little tired, so I decided to end early. I planned to be in Florida tomorrow, where I'd stay in Jacksonville with a couple I'd made contact with through warmshowers.org. Today I passed the two-thousand-mile mark. I had a hard time believing I'd traveled two thousand miles under my own power.

CHAPTER SEVEN

Florida, Part One

Day Sixty-Five; August 25, 2010
Woodbine, Georgia, to Jacksonville,
Florida—68.1 Miles

I had arranged through warmshowers.org to stay with Faye in
Jacksonville. The day was warm and wonderful. The road was
lined with Spanish-moss covered trees. I had come to love the
quite back roads of Georgia and was sorry to leave them behind.
I crossed the Florida border early in the day. It was a confusing
crossing for me. I was very excited to be in Florida, but I was
feeling anxious about the impending end of the trip. I had come
to realize that I was not ready to stop biking. An idea had been
rolling around in head for a while. At first it was just a passing
thought, but the idea had taken on a life of its own. I was, slowly
and somewhat reluctantly, coming to the conclusion the road
was not done with me. Why not just turn west? There were still
a lot of roads to ride.

The landscape took a sudden change as I explored the first few miles of Florida. Gothic trees covered with Spanish moss quickly yielded to Palm trees. The world that I was moving through was fast becoming a lush tropical one. When I crossed the sign for the city limits of Jacksonville, I looked left, then right. Seeing nothing but undeveloped wet land was a pleasant surprise. The land north of Jacksonville was wet and beautiful.

I rejoined route one in the middle of Jacksonville. We had been separated for a while; it was comforting to be back with her. We were old lovers reunited. We held each other for a minute, smiled and started the next leg of our adventure.

The clouds took on a vague threating look as I left the middle of the city. I called Faye, the women I was staying with to update her on my progress. I made it to her development before any real rain started Faye had held dinner for me. She was an exemplary hostess. The home cooked meal was delicious, warm and filling. She and her dogs, Nugget and Dusty, made me feel welcomed. They treated me as if IK was a family member, not guest. The bed was soft and sung. Sleep captured me with ease.

Day Sixty-Six; August 26, 2010

Jacksonville, Florida, to Palm Coast,

Florida—Sixty-One Miles

Today will live in infamy. The day got off to a great start. Faye made me scrambled eggs with cheese and onions. She made me feel like I was the only guest in a very exclusive B and B. She also mixed me up an electrolyte drink that she uses. Her kindness and generosity were remarkable.

I biked to St. Augustine, where I almost join the armadillos. A truck driver rolled through a stop sign as I came through an intersection. The very blue, very big grill was the only thing I could see. It was so immense that it blocked out the sun and became the center of my universe. I was mere inches from being a fifteen-second story on the St. Augustine evening news. I used my secret superpower, the ability to scream, "F-ing stop!" at ten thousand decibels. The truck driver stopped, and my scream shattered everything made of crystal within a five-block radius. I was very angry but also relieved.

The next issue was my trailer tire, which went flat. Try as I might, I couldn't find the leak. I pumped the tire and headed to a bike shop Faye had recommended. My iPad gave me excellent directions. They would have worked, except they went through a gated community, where a crazy guy on a bike definitely wasn't allowed. I biked around St. Augustine for what seemed like hours, looking for the bike shop. I was about to give up and drag my trailer to the next town, when I finally found the shop. In no time I changed out my tube and was back on the road.

The third issue of the day was quickly upon me. It started to rain, which wasn't the issue. The rain started to come down hard; I stopped outside a convenience store to wait out the worst of it. While I was waiting, I got a sudden, severe call of nature, which I couldn't ignore. I knew it was going to be more than a brief visit to the bathroom. I asked the clerk if I could bring my bike and trailer inside and have him watch it. He was fine with letting me bring everything inside. As I pushed the bike into the store, however, the bungee cord that secured my bag to the trailer got wrapped around the trailer wheel. I sprinted to the bathroom to avoid an embarrassing and unsightly event. After finishing up in the bathroom, I returned to the store proper. I had to lie on the floor and untangle the Gordian knot that my bungee cord had become. I didn't have to resort to Alexander's sword solution to dislodge the cord from the wheel, but I did consider it.

The next and final issue of the day was a hurricane brewing off the coast. I could see the storm clouds creeping toward me. I secured everything as well as I could and headed down the road again. The rain hit me with a fierce, sudden, salty fury at a ninety-degree angle. It was so hard that it stung like hail. I was forced to pull over because I couldn't see. I huddled at the side of the road until the worst of it was over. During a pause in the storm, I biked to a small motel and took shelter under the stairwell. That's when I discovered that the new tube in the trailer tire had been punctured. That was the straw that broke the camel's back. I limped to the office and got a room for the night.

Day Sixty-Seven; August 27, 2010

Palm Coast, Florida, to Ponce Inlet,

Florida—Approximately Forty Miles

I took it very, very easy today. I biked about forty miles to a Ponce Inlet, just south of Daytona. I was amazed at how cheap the motel rooms were. Beachfront rooms were priced as low as forty dollars; across the street from the ocean they cost twenty-five dollars. I was staying in a vacation condo owned by friends of my brother-in-law and his wife. As I biked into Ponce Inlet, I had one of my very few negative interactions with a car. A twenty-something kid riding in the back of a pickup yelled at me to ride on the sidewalk. For some reason it really irritated me, and I yelled back for him to shut up or come back and make me. I must look more frightening than I thought. He shut up and turned around to face the front of the truck so fast that I thought his head would spin off. All of my anger vanished, and I had to laugh.

The condo was another example of how generous people can be. The owners were people I never had met. That didn't, however, prevent them from opening their place to me.

Days Sixty-Eight and Sixty-Nine; August 28–29, 2010

Ponce Inlet, Florida—Rest Days

My brother-in-law Bob and his wife Mary and their daughter Nicky came over from Tampa for the day. Their other two kids, Bobby and Kim, college students in Orlando, drove over also. Bobby brought his girlfriend, Amanda. It was a mini family reunion. I was a little anxious because they're Nan's relatives. My fears, however, were groundless. All of my anxiety melted away when I saw them. They had been my family for twenty-four years, and the prospect of losing them would have been more than I could bear.

We went to an outdoor restaurant/bar, DJ's Deck, for shrimp and beer in Daytona Beach. Then we moved on to Crabby Joe's, right on the ocean, for lunch. The food was outstanding; I had a yellow fin tuna sandwich and more beer.

Bob is the sort of person who always knows the best places to go; he's a born tour guide. It doesn't matter if it's food, beer, or music; he's the authority. He also has an outgoing personality, which, coupled with his very generous tipping, ensures that every water and waitress always remembers him. After our day on the town in Daytona, we returned to Ponce Inlet. We came back to the condo for a bit then went to the beach for the afternoon. The hurricane offshore was producing massive waves. I played in the water like I was a little kid; the water just washing away, for a time, my worries. At one point I found myself way offshore, away from everyone. I was all by myself, but it was all right.

Day Seventy—August 30, 2010

Ponce Inlet, Florida, to Melbourne, Florida—84.5 Miles

After spending a decadent couple of days of resting, I was ready to get on the road—almost. When I woke up at seven, it was raining and very windy. I looked out the window, grunted, rolled over, and went back to sleep. I awoke again at 9:20 a.m. This time I was able to drag myself out of bed. I packed my bag, closed up the condo, and hit the road.

I had some hotel points left over on a credit card from a past life, so I booked a room in Melbourne, Florida. It was a nice, long ride. I knew I wouldn't wimp out. I was just too cheap to lose a free night in a hotel.

The weather was excellent for biking—overcast and not too hot. I came to love overcast days on this part of the trip. Early in the day, I passed a motel that was surrounded by police and reporters. One of the rooms was cordoned off with yellow crime-scene tape. I was pretty sure I was passing a murder scene (it turned out I was right). I thought about stopping to join the other rubberneckers, but I didn't want to end up being a person of interest again.

A few miles down the road, I realized I had forgotten to put on my sunscreen and butt butter. The sunscreen wasn't too much of an issue; I had the best tan of my life. The butt butter, however, was a real issue. My rear end was bothering me, so I pulled over behind a carwash. I was really hoping no one had seen me with a tube of cream in one hand and the other in my pants...

As I stood there, a severe stomach cramp hit me, and I had to dash into the woods. I spotted a gas station bathroom not more than fifty feet away, but I couldn't even make it that short distance, so I squatted in sparse cover. Fortunately I didn't make the police blotter that day. I think I had too much watermelon during my stay at Ponce Inlet.

I could see the ocean for much of the trip; it was very soothing. I had a very odd perception of the ride today. I kept feeling that I was not making good time, but at the end of the day I had a new record 84.5

Total miles 2234 miles to date for the trip. 330 miles to Key West was just 330 miles away.

Day Seventy-One; August 31, 2010

Melbourne, Florida, to Vero Beach,

Florida—39.6 Miles

I slept very late. I think the previous day without sunscreen really took a toll on me. I started the day with an early light lunch at Hooters, my new favorite restaurant. Then I went to a bike shop for some supplies, extra tubes, and some biking food. I meet a biker who was riding a BMX bike that had been modified into a recumbent bike.

I detoured onto Florida State Road A1A, where I spotted two gopher tortoises, their large domed shells were very different then the turtles of Vermont. I enjoyed watching them lumbering through the vegetation at the side of the road. I stopped to talk with a police officer to ask a question, and she asked to see my ID. It was a good thing that I didn't have any outstanding warrants. A little while later, another tour biker stopped to chat with me. Chris Miller was biking from Providence, Rhode Island, to Key West to raise money for Meals on Wheels. I was amazed at how light he was traveling. He had almost no gear—just a small bivy sack and the clothes on his back. On top of that, his bicycle was a bottom-of-the-line department store mountain bike. He was making incredible time — eighty-plus miles a day. I've kept track of Chris ever since. After this trip he did a through-hike of the Appalachian Trail. Chris told me he was staying at an ocean-front house for the night, courtesy of couchsurfing.org. I crossed back onto Route 1 and stopped at Vero Beach for the night.

Day Seventy-Two; September 1, 2010
Vero Beach, Florida, to Stuart,
Florida—About Thirty-Two Miles

I slept great last night. In the morning I started with the intention of reaching Palm Beach, a little less than seventy miles from Vero Beach. Alas, the biking and trailer gods decided otherwise. The trailer tire blew; then I fixed it and was back on the road. A few miles down the road, my chain broke. The last time I'd had a chain break was in the 1960s. I ended up pushing my bike to the nearest bike shop, which was about three away miles. They were busy, and it took a while to get the bike fixed. I had them replace the chain, but I kept the old one as a backup. After I left the shop, I biked a little while and started to see spots, so I listened to my body and called it a day. The last few days, I'd felt very tired but not as bad as I had in South Carolina; I was just feeling rundown.

Day Seventy-Three; September 2, 2010
Stuart, Florida, to Lantana,
Florida—Forty-Seven Miles

I felt better today than I did the last couple of days, even though I got a late start. It was very hot today, but the sky was a beautiful blue, and there wasn't a cloud in the sky. The ocean was on my left for much of the day. I found myself getting lost in the ocean views. At one point I met a very nice man who was riding a thirty-year-old Schwinn cruiser. I spent a few minutes talking with him. At the end of our conversation, I gave him my card. At first he thought I was trying to sell him something or had some sort of an angle. He seemed genuinely surprised when he found out I wasn't after his money.

Key West—266 miles and counting.

Day Seventy-Four; September 3, 2010
Lantana, Florida, to North Miami,
Florida—Fifty Miles

It was hot as usual today, and then it started rain. At first it was just a few drops, then a full-fledged downpour assaulted me. The rainwater overcame the road drainage, and soon the highway was more like a Venice canal than a roadway. The rain came down so hard that I had to get off the road because I couldn't see. When a car passed, it would send a small tidal wave at me. I took refuge in a little Brazilian restaurant. This was the first time I'd ever had Brazilian food. It was delicious, filling, and cheap. When I left the restaurant, the rain had let up, but the road was still covered in water. It was so deep that the when cars passed me they made waves that were high enough to surf on. I had to get up on the sidewalk and get as far away from the road as possible to keep from being swamped.

As I entered the Miami area, most of the signs were in Spanish, and Spanish music blared out of the stereos of passing cars. I heard rapid-fire Spanish spoken on every street corner; I felt a little like a visitor in a foreign land. I checked into a cheap hotel with bars on every window. The clerk gave me a close appraisal. When I told him I wanted a single room, he said, "I'd better not see anyone else going into your room." I replied, "If you do, someone will be breaking in, so call the police." I earned a small wry smile for my effort.

I felt very close now. The thought of being almost to Key West made me feel proud. Without a doubt I knew I would finish the trip. I was excited but also a little scared. I thought I'd have things in better focus; I thought I'd be sure of what I wanted to do next, but I wasn't. The feeling that I wasn't through with biking had been creeping up on me for a while.

Day Seventy-Five; September 4, 2010
North Miami, Florida, to Florida City,
Florida—38.2 Miles

Miami drivers had claimed the much coveted title as the worst drivers of the trip. They had no concern for me at all. I wanted to shake them and scream, "Don't you understand how much paperwork there will be if you hit me?" They kept passing me with two or three inches to spare. I could read the time off their watches. I thought about escaping to the sidewalk, but the pedestrian traffic was too heavy.

I found a great trail in Key Biscayne—the trail that parallels US Route 1 all the way to Florida City. It was such a relief to be in an auto-free zone. Much of the trail was under the highway, which protected me from the sun. The homeless were evident along much of the path. I saw one-person campsites as well as small groups banded together. I was hailed several times with shouts of "God bless" from people who were indigent. Covered with street grime, toothless, or nearly toothless, they were kinder than the SUV and Mercedes drivers of the city.

I got to Florida City with plenty of light left in the day. This was the last stop on the mainland before the Keys. I got some fluids and rested outside a convenience store that was doing brisk business; suitcases of beer flew off the shelves, and six-packs were a close second. Most of these beers were headed down Route 1 to the Keys. Did I hear the familiar sound of pop tops as the drivers pulled out of the parking lot? I'm pretty sure I did.

Starting again down Route 1, I passed the Last Chance Saloon, a well-known bar. I thought about stopping but passed and continued along. The road was good for about a mile. Then I hit construction. It also started to rain, and the shoulder disappeared. The traffic was heavy. My mind went back to the convenience store. How many people, racing down this road, on a Saturday night, on a holiday weekend, may have started their Keys vacation a little early? How many tops had been popped? I decided to backtrack to Florida City and get a room for the night. I also decided I was done camping on this trip; I was tired of sleeping on the ground.

Day Seventy-Six; September 5, 2010

Florida City, Florida, to Layton, Florida—61.2 Miles

It was a very wise choice to turn back last night. The road was flat, but there was a ton of traffic, and I had very little shoulder to play with. I soon discovered that all the people who were super laidback and relaxed in Key West drove like the Devil was chasing them to get there. I can't claim that anyone broke the sound barrier while passing me, but they were close. I skipped breakfast this morning because I wanted to eat my first meal today in the Keys. When I reached Key Largo, I was plenty hungry.

I stopped for a late breakfast/early lunch at Mrs. Mac's Kitchen. Nan and I had taken our last trip as a couple to the Keys. We had breakfast at Mrs. Mac's several times; the eggs Benedict are to die for. It was the obligatory trip many couples make when they know the end is nigh but they can't let go. We stayed at the Key Lime Sailing Club in Key Largo, the perfect romantic getaway. It's right on the water and has neat little cottages. We stayed in a cottage at the edge of the water and took a glass-bottom boat tour of the coral reef. We rented kayaks and paddled out and around a small mangrove-covered island. We followed a small ray around the bay. Nan painted her toenails red. We drank, ate, and played in the sun. At times it felt strained and a little forced, but I thought we were having a good time. Later Nan told me she had felt lost on the trip. I think I knew it while we were there but just couldn't face it.

We went to the movies one night. We arrived early. It was a warm, beautiful summer evening, and we walked around while we waited for the movie to start. I remember feeling an incredibly powerful bittersweet sadness. In my heart of hearts, I knew we were done, but I was happy to have that last little bit of time with her.

I had very mixed feelings about nearing the end of my bike trip. I was happy to be closing in on my goal but sad that I was almost done. It turned out that I was only approaching the halfway point of the trip.

I reached Layton, Florida, on Long Key, feeling tired and a little sad. The end of the trip and the memories of the last time I was here were taking a toll on me. I'm a little ashamed to say I was feeling sorry for myself. I would soon learn that no matter how bad you have it, there's always someone who would kill to have your life.

There weren't a lot of options for a room for the night. I spotted the Lime Tree Bay Resort, and with some trepidation, I decided to check it out. I was certain they'd want all of my money and my left kidney for a room. I must have touched something in the clerk when she saw me. She seemed to take pity on the fifty-three-year-old waif who had appeared at her counter. They don't get a lot of bicyclists stopping at the resort, and the rack rate was well beyond what I was willing to pay. The clerk gave me the super-saver-depressed-biker-who-arrives-late discount. She let me have a spacious room facing the sunset at an almost ridiculous rate.

We talked for a while about my trip, and she opened up about her life. She had been married for twenty years to an alcoholic. She had stuck with him through good and mostly bad times. Finally he got sober, but her joy was short-lived. Within a few months, he left her for another woman. She survived, packed up her life, and moved to the Keys. While she was putting her life back together, she discovered she had breast cancer. She successfully fought off the cancer, then found a man, loved again, remarried, and was happy. He dropped dead eighteen months later. She still, at least on the outside, had an awesome attitude. I thought about her that night; it helped me get over feeling sorry for myself.

Day Seventy-Seven; September 6, 2010

Layton, Florida, to Key West, Florida—68.2 Miles

Yesterday I passed the 2,500-mile mark. That number is staggering. A year ago I wouldn't have believed you if you'd said

I'd bike fifty miles in one day; now I was a little more than fifty miles from Key West.

It was a fantastic day to finish the trip. Clear, sunny skies and warm breezes made me feel like I had died and gone to tour bikers' heaven. The Keys are simply beautiful. To someone who had lived in the Northeast all his life, they have an exotic feel. The palm trees are something out of a dream. Tiny crabs appear out nowhere, shuttling sideways at a rapid pace in front of me. The little lizards that darted across my path had an almost alien feel. Even their names — gecko, anole, skink — evoke an other-worldly feel to me. The lizards increased in size as I got closer to Key West. It seemed gradual, but I soon realized they were no longer tiny little toy-like reptiles. They were getting very large — two and three feet long! I finally realized they were Iguanas. Iguanas aren't native to Florida, but it was apparent that they were now well established here.

I arrived at the Seven Mile Bridge full of excitement. It connects Knights Key (part of the city of Marathon, Florida) in the Middle Keys to Little Duck Key in the Lower Keys. I've always loved bridges. The prospect of riding my bicycle over one that was seven miles long was exhilarating. There are actually two seven-mile-long bridges here. The old bridge, which was extensively damaged several times over the years, is still there. The new bridge was built from 1978 to 1982. Motor vehicles are no longer allowed on the old bridge; I had read horror stories about riding a bike across it back when cars were allowed on it. It's more like a lane-and-a-half than two lanes. With very little room for even two cars passing, it was a feat of daring to ride a bike across it. I started down the old bridge, thinking I'd avoid the car traffic on the new bridge.

Shortly after starting down the old bridge, I noticed two women walking toward me. One seemed unsteady on her feet. When we met I stopped to speak with them. They were a mother and a daughter. It was the daughter who was unsteady on her feet. She had been in a horrific auto accident years previously. Her mother had dedicated her life to nursing her make to health. The daughter had one of the most amazing smiles I'd ever seen.

When I was in her presence, I felt like I was speaking with an angel. She radiated a feeling of love and kindness, despite the fact that she was wearing a New York Yankees baseball cap. There was a little crack in her angelic armor when she learned I was a Red Sox fan. She gave me a playful punch to my shoulder, which I still treasure. If the girl was an angel, her mother was an archangel. She had given up everything to care for her child. She had ignored a dim medical prognosis and given her a daughter a joyful life. The connection between them was incredible, and it was awe inspiring to have met them. It also saved me a little time and embarrassment; the old bridge only goes as far as Pigeon Island. I said my goodbyes, turned around, and headed for the new bridge. The new bridge turned out to be a great ride, with wide shoulders and stunning views. It was one of the highlights of the trip.

The closer I got to Key West, the harder the biking got. I don't think it was physical; my emotions were just riding very high. I didn't have a nervous breakdown, but it was a close thing. On the lighter side, I did sing at the top of my lungs "It's Five O'Clock Somewhere" — well, at least the lines "Pour me something tall and strong. Make it a hurricane before I go insane." I made it to mile marker zero with my sanity mostly intact, but my arrival was a bit anticlimactic. Maybe I was expecting there to be a banner for me to bike through with my hands thrown up in the air and a crowd cheering, "Ed! Ed! Ed!" but in the end it was just me and my bike. There is in fact nothing at mile marker zero, except the mile marker itself.

I asked a couple to take my picture; they looked at me, turned their heads away, and kept walking. I barely managed to keep myself from breaking out in maniacal laughter; I didn't get the hero's greeting I'd hoped for. I did manage to get a group of four young women to stop and take my picture. They oohed and aahed over me a little, but any fantasies were soon quashed. They were in fact two couples, and they played for the other team. I biked from mile marker zero to Duval Street and stopped at the first open-air bar I came to, the Flying Monkey. I had a drink and spoke with the bartender. He listened to my tale of biking from

Fort Kent, Maine, to Key West. He bought me my second drink and proceeded to tell me about his roommates. They had started in Portland, Oregon, then bicycled to New York and then down the coast to Key West. I guess if I was going to really impress anyone, I'd have to keep going.

Day Seventy-Nine; September 8, 2010

Key West, Florida, to Fort Myers, Florida—by Ferry

I spent a couple of days in Key West; it was perfect, and I was very close to never leaving. The end-of-the-road feel was just what I craved. The city was full of breathtaking sunsets, dazzling scenery, and alluring women. There was food everywhere and enough alcohol to kill every living thing in the world. And did I say alluring women? My time there was short, and most of the stories will stay in Key West. I will say that I had a great time.

My plan had been to ride my bike to Orlando to catch a plane to North Carolina. There I would meet up with Bradley, Joel, and Jessica. We were planning to ride together to Virginia for my niece Katie's wedding. Mary, my sister-in-law, messaged me and offered to let me stay with her and her family in Lutz, Florida, for a few days. They would clean me up, feed me, and give me a ride to the airport. I changed my plans and purchased a ticket on the Key West express ferry, which ran between Key West and Fort Myers. Mary planned on picking me up the next day.

I got on the ferry in Key West feeling great. I had biked 2,500 miles—the entire length of the East Coast. Now I was heading to join my relatives in Tampa for a few days of hot food, clean sheets, warm showers, and cold, cold beer. I was heading for Nirvana. The first hint that the day held a few unexpected twists and turns came at the security checkpoint. The ferry terminal at Key West is federally run, which means it has the same security as airports. While they were searching my bag, they made an announcement. The security guard held up my trusty hand axe and said, "We would consider this a weapon." Sheepishly I owned up to my weapon; graciously they didn't taser me. They even agreed to return my axe at the end of the trip. Getting on the ferry was a bit of a pain. I had to pay for myself, my bike, and my trailer. Finding space to store everything on the ship was a little awkward but nothing life changing. After I stowed everything away, I was ready to relax for the trip.

The ferry from Key West to Fort Myers was amazing. It was a triple-decker, with a full bar and cable TV—a giant floating 747. Moving on the water at so fast was like being on the *Starship Enterprise*. We made it to Fort Myers at around 9:30 p.m. I was very excited; I was staying at a very cool little B and B, the kind that leaves the light on and the door open. I was planning on a relaxing night of watching bad TV. Ah, the best-laid plans of mice and bicyclists. The night was going to take an abrupt turn. As we were disembarking, the crew informed me that I needed to be the last one off. It made perfect sense; getting my bicycle, the trailer, and my gear was an involved process. I was happy to let everyone go ahead of me. I'd have a very short ride to the B and B; the night was beautiful; and I was fat and happy.

The crew helped me off the ship and asked me if I was OK. I told them I was, and they rushed back on the ferry to get it ready for its next trip. It was apparent that they were on a tight schedule.

I balanced my bike against a piling on the deck while I attached my trailer to the rear tire. This turned out to be a serious, nearly fatal mistake. As I straddled the trailer and started to connect it to the bike, I lost my balance. It was just a small slip but enough to cause the trailer to bump into my right leg. That was the start of the falling of the dominoes that sent me on a dramatic mini adventure. I reached out to stabilize myself with the netting that stretched from piling to piling. To my surprise the netting was simply there for show, as a warning to the dimwitted that they should go no farther. It was in no way intended to prevent anyone from falling into the water. As I started my downward trajectory, toward the canal below, with the flimsy netting grasped futilely in my hands, I almost giggled at the stupidity of the position I was in. The netting would briefly hold then would tear off the staple. It would catch on the next staple, hold briefly, and again tear. I lathered, rinsed, and repeated until I was upside-down and headed for the drink.

As I fell off the dock, the ten thousand times I had awoken from a dream of drowning flashed through my mind. On the way down, I passed a rope on the wall; I was really hoping my foot wouldn't get tangled and hang me upside-down with my head underwater. I didn't have the abs to save myself if that happened. Your perception of time really does slowdown in these situations. I thought about my kids. I thought about a girl I had met in Key West. And, incredibly, I thought about how long it would take me to get to my room for the night! I wondered whether this was the end of my journey — and my life. How ironic would it be to drown on a bicycle? But what a great ending this would be to my book, if I could complete it from beyond my watery grave.

I hit the water headfirst. Then I had a moment of clarity. If I didn't panic, I wouldn't drown. I righted myself and kicked for the surface. Just before I broke the surface, the bike trailer I had pulled from Maine to Florida — the trailer that had been my faithful sidekick — came down on top of me, landing directly on my head. I don't believe inanimate objects have thoughts or feelings or plans, but at that moment, I hated the ungrateful little bastard.

I got out from under the trailer and broke the surface. I was able to hold the trailer on the surface with one hand and grab a piling with the other. Now, when people tell you that barnacles are sharp, they're not kidding. Although I didn't feel any pain, the fingers of my left hand were torn all to hell.

Looking around I could see no way out of the water — no ladder, no ramp, and no people anywhere. I was in water over my head; holding on to a barnacle piling that was performing major surgery on my left hand, while trying to keep my trailer afloat with my other hand. Suddenly I realized I was dripping blood into the water. I was off the beaten path for bull sharks, but I was doing a pretty good job advertising for the late-night all-the-Ed-Bradley-you-can-eat buffet.

You never really want to be in the position where you find yourself yelling, "Help! Help me!" for real. When you get to the point where you yell, "Please help me!" you know you're in real trouble. In the back of your brain, a little voice is telling you no one will come if you're not polite. That's just what I did, as if people were just standing around on the dock saying, "How rude. Did no one teach that man to use the magic word?" I may have even added a "God, please help me" at that point. I wondered whether this was it for the off-off-Broadway production of the *Ed Bradley Show*. Would this be the final curtain call?

Finally a head appeared over the edge of the dock. A deckhand told me he and his coworkers could hear me, but they couldn't find me. He didn't add, "We never thought to look over the edge of the dock. No one could be that stupid." They produced a hook that they used to fish my trailer out of the canal. Then they tossed a rope over the edge of the dock. I half-climbed it while they dragged me; I made it about three-fourths of the way to the top before I lost my grip. I slid down the side of the dock, shedding skin at an alarming rate. On the second attempt, they got me onto the dock. There I lay, happy to be alive. Was I embarrassed? Sure, but it was a good embarrassed.

My body wasn't a pretty sight. The fingers on my left hand were slashed from the barnacles. My arms and legs were cut, bruised, and abraded. I looked like I'd been through a Cuisinart on the human-puree level. I just lay on the hard, warm, dry deck, breathing heavily in and out. It felt like a feather bed in a five-star hotel. After a few minutes of respite, the captain gave me the bad news. Because of the toxins in the water, they would have to pour bleach into my wounds. They stripped me down and proceeded to pour bleach into every open wound on my body. Boys and girls, you haven't lived until you've had bleached poured into your wounds. No need to waterboard our enemies—just a little steel-wool rubdown and household bleach will do the trick. I think I may have confessed to the Lindbergh baby kidnapping. On a brighter note, after they had properly hosed me off, they gave me a free T-shirt.

They took me back on the ship to complete the paperwork for my ordeal. There's always paperwork. I signed blindly; my glasses were casualties of my late-night dip. Who knows—it's possible that I signed myself into indentured servitude. After declining a trip in an ambulance, I attached my trailer to the bike. This time I had the crew's help.

I rode away into the darkness of Fort Myers and made it to my room for the night. It was a small bed and breakfast, and they indeed had left my door open for me. As I walked into my room, I noticed bright-red spots on the floor. I thought it was a very irregular and unusual pattern for tile. It took a few seconds for me to realize that the "pattern" on the tile was blood dripping from the wounds on my hand; they had started to bleed again on the ride from the dock. Using most of the towels and washcloths provided for me, I managed to stanch the bleeding. After I was done, it looked like I had butchered a small pig in the bathroom. I tossed and turned while trying in vain to fall asleep. Finally I drifted off at around 5:00 a.m. for a few hours. I was glad to be alive.

Day Eighty; September 9, 2010

Fort Myers, Florida, to Lutz,

Florida—via Automobile

The next morning I was in a tremendous amount of pain. Abrasions and bruises covered my arms and legs. The fingers of my left hand had been sliced and diced; they were gruesome to look at. I managed to shower, but it was far from delightful. My cell phone, which had endured the trials and tribulations of the entire length of the East Coast, hadn't survived the night. The salt water had turned it into a paperweight. Not having phone communication with Mary was problematic. I ended up using Facebook to contact my daughter Jenny, who called Mary to work out the details of my extraction. We planned to rendezvous at the ferry parking lot, which was just a short bike ride away for me.

The fingers of my left hand, however, couldn't grip the handle-bar. I couldn't close my left hand; my fingers weren't capable of that motion. My legs also felt miserable. My right leg had a deep indentation from where it had hit the dock on my way down. My appendages could make the necessary motions to bike, but they were far from happy. The trip back to the scene of the accident was painful but mercifully short. My sunglasses, the flag to my trailer, and a few other items were missing in action. I did a short search on the dock without success. Swallowing my pride, I went to the office and asked whether they had found any of my gear. I was greeted as a minor celebrity (or a major idiot). "Hey, you're the guy who fell off the dock!" were the first words out of everyone's mouths. None of my equipment had been found. I thanked them and slunk away to wait for Mary.

Mary's arrival with her truck was cause for a small celebration. We loaded the bike, the trailer, and the rest of my gear and were off. It had been more than a month since I had been in a car, and the motion again felt strange. The speed was disorientating. Two-and-a-half hours later, we were at Bob and Mary's house in Lutz, Florida. They lived in a gated community, right next to a PGA golf course. In less than twenty-four hours, I had gone from nearly drowning in dirty canal water to drinking beer at the tiki bar on their lanai. Life takes some strange bounces.

While I was staying in Lutz with Bob and Mary, we went to the Yard, a musical venue in Tampa. Its name perfectly defines it; it's the backyard of Mark and Sharon Leverett. They constructed a stage and regularly hold concerts there. Most of the artists who perform there are well respected members of the trop-rock world. Trop rock is a combination of calypso, Caribbean, folk, country, rock 'n' roll, and reggae, with a little zydeco thrown in. Jimmy Buffet is probably the best-known performer of the genre. The Yard is a small, intimate place. You are right on top of the artists, sometimes literally. It's a BYOB and bring-a-dish-to-pass venue. A card table at the door takes your donation and passes out raffle tickets. The alcohol flows early, freely, and often, and there's a great deal of gratuitous hugging by the end of the evening. I felt like a member of the family almost immediately. Scattered around the yard are tree stumps with the names of regulars carved into them. Early in the night, they serve as tables for drinks. Later they're mini stages for guests to dance on. Much later they're obstacles to trip over as you attempt to dance. Everyone dances. People dance with the lack of inhibition that comes from the trop-rock music, as well as the copious amounts of alcohol imbibed with friends, new and old. They dance with the lack of inhibition that comes from being in the dark, with the lack of inhibition that comes from being in a place without judgment.

Mike Miller was singing one of the nights we were there and became my new favorite performer within seconds. He sang a song that I came to love, even though it brings me to tears every time I hear it. It's a conversation between two men in a bar. One is the owner of a sailboat that's for rent; the other is an old man who wants to charter it. Life has taken a hard turn for the old man.

"he came home to find his wife all packed.
She took him for everything… She even took the confidence he lacked.

The refrain is beautiful and haunting. It captures so exquisitely, so painfully, what I felt.

I wanna take your boat as far as it goes, feel Jamaican sand between my toes.
I wanna ride on the wind just as far as I can.
I won't be any trouble to haul… I can sleep anywhere at all.
And I don't eat very much for a hollow man.
I wanna ride on the wind just as far as I can.
I won't be any trouble to haul… I can sleep anywhere at all.
And I don't eat very much for a hollow man."

That's what I was doing. I was going to ride the wind as far as I could go.

CHAPTER EIGHT

Florida, Part Two

Day 113; October 12, 2010

Lutz, Florida

I got my hair cut for the new leg of the trip at Tats and Cuts Barbershop. I had driven by the strip mall where it was located several times while I was staying with Bob and Mary in Lutz, Florida. I had been drawn to the place. It was a combination tattoo parlor/barbershop. For some reason I felt compelled to have my hair cut there. The shop was very well kept up. I had thought of tattoo parlors as places to get hepatitis C and ill-conceived messages inked onto your body. This place was far from that. It was clean and sleek, and the décor was dominated by chrome and dark shades. It was much different than I had expected. The barbershop was in the back left coroner.

The owner was younger than me, probably in his mid-thirties. He was slight of build and baby faced and had short-cropped brown hair. He was equal parts showman and barber. Getting my hair cut was much more of an event than I was used to. He was very personable and made me feel at ease right away. We talked about depression and how hard life can be sometimes. He'd had to downsize from a larger shop and had lost his house due to financial problems. He spoke about his personal and family issues with deep emotion. In support of my trip, he ended up giving me a free haircut. He also joined my Facebook page while I was in his shop. At the time I didn't know that he would be my third of four connections with violent death on the trip. The rest of the story, as Paul Harvey would say, was slightly different.

After finishing up the bike trip in San Diego, I returned to visit with the barbershop owner. I wanted to get my hair cut and catch up with him. I went back to the strip mall where his business had been. The shop looked different from the outside. Shrugging my shoulders, I walked inside. The space had been transformed. It now looked like a barbershop from the 1950s. Everything was white, and the place was filled with light. An edgy tattoo artist had replaced the middle-aged men in white smocks. I wouldn't have been surprised to see Andy Griffith sitting in the chair next to me. I sat in the chair to get my hair cut. Asking the barber what had happened to the owner got me a few seconds of silence. Then he said, with a sigh, "That boy sure could cut hair," with grudging respect.

After another pause he told me what had happened. The previous owner had gotten into legal trouble that involved drugs. He had come into the shop one night and stripped everything of value, all of which was still missing; he had hidden or sold all of it. Then he had gone to his estranged girlfriend's house and shot and killed her. Shortly after he drove away from the scene, a police car pulled up behind him. Apparently he thought they were after him, so he sped away. The officer reacted and followed him. After a short chase, the man lost control of his car and crashed into an abandoned house, where his vehicle exploded and he burned to death. I was stunned. It made me wonder how many people have some sort of darkness beneath the surface that we never see.

Day 115; October 14, 2010

Lutz, Florida, to Fort Myers, Florida—by Car

Fort Myers, Florida, to Key West, Florida—by Ferry

I was up very early to catch the ferry. Mary had agreed to drive me back to the scene of the crime. It was hard to leave the warmth of the Noble family. I even had considered staying in the Tampa area. There were plenty of hospitals where I could work. Living near the Nobles would have been very comfortable. I would've had family nearby and a turn-key social life. I tried on the idea of getting a job and an apartment. When I started to think about it, however, my body reacted. My head ached. My stomach felt like it was going to empty itself. I was afraid I'd start running in circles and baying at themoon like a drunken dog. There was no way I could stay there and not have gone insane.

It was still dark when we packed my bicycle and gear into the back of their truck. We left the neighborhood quietly. I felt a little pang of something close to homesickness. The roads weren't quite empty as we passed through Tampa. As we crossed the bridge, out of town, the lights of the city were beautiful. Something about lights over the water always makes me feel warm inside. I dozed off during the ride; riding in cars always has put me to sleep. We got to Fort Myers with plenty of time to spare. Mary helped me unload the truck, and we said our goodbyes. It wouldn't be long before I saw her again; my plan was to bike from Key West, through the Everglades, and up the Gulf Coast, back to Tampa. I was worried I might be on a "no sail" list because of my late-night swim the last time I had ridden the ferry. My worry was for nothing; no one blinked an eye.

Day 117; October 16, 2010

Key West, Florida, to Marathon City,

Florida—51.5 Miles

After two days of playing in Key West, I resumed my journey. I was headed north, for the first time on the trip. The entire ride today, I felt like the ocean was on the wrong side. I had decided not to camp on this mini leg of the trip, so I left my trailer in Lutz with Bob and Mary. I was just using a backpack until I got back to their house. It did cause me some neck pain and back pain, but I moved a lot faster. It was warm, but not too warm, as I left Key West. At the start of the day, I also had solid a headwind to contend with.

It felt great to be on the road again. My body did complain, especially my rear end, after my prolonged break. I also felt some mild tightness in my legs, but otherwise I felt strong. I didn't leave Key West until after one thirty; I didn't want to leave. I really thought about getting a job and staying there.

On the ride I saw a Key deer. It looked like a miniature version of the white-tailed deer I was so familiar with from Vermont.

I crossed over the Seven Mile Bridge again. It was just as spectacular the second time.

Day 118; October 17, 2010

Marathon City, Florida, to Islamorada, Florida—30.5 Miles

Today was physically tough for me. My back hurt, probably from wearing the backpack. My butt cheeks also were very sore from the layoff. Sweating off the alcohol I'd consumed over the last few weeks was more painful than I'd thought it would be. I finally stopped to rest in Islamorada. I lay down beside the road and closed my eyes for what I thought would be a few seconds. An hour later I woke up as if I'd been hibernating. I was still exhausted. I was very surprised I hadn't been awakened by the authorities. Fortunately I had fallen asleep across the street from a motel. I pushed my bike over there and checked in for the night.

Day 119; October 18, 2010

Islamorada, Florida, to Florida City, Florida—45.6 Miles

The day started out better physically for me. My butt cheeks were only whining today, and the weather held out nicely. As I closed in on Florida City, however, my back started to spasm. I stopped at mile marker 117 to lie on my back to try to loosen up my muscles. It worked, but my relief was short-lived. Three miles down the road, the spasms drove me off the bike again.

While I was lying down at mile marker 120, Miami-Dade Fire Rescue showed up. Someone had called me in as a man down! Right behind them was the sheriff. They seemed a little disappointed that I was OK. I got the feeling they were having a slow day and were a little bored. The sheriff did tell me it would be safer to bike on the other side of the road, which was closed for construction. He watched for traffic as I hopped over the retaining wall. The whole experience was so different from yesterday, when people had calmly ignored or tolerated me as I slept roadside. Despite all the excitement and physical ailments, I arrived in Florida City in great spirits and had made good time. Tomorrow I would be in the Everglades, a lifelong goal.

Day 120; October 19, 2010

Florida City, Florida, to Everglade City,

Florida—83.3 Miles

The day started with a flat; I patched it and headed north. My back and butt felt much better today. Still I was having a hard time getting into a groove at the beginning of the day.

I sat outside a convenience store at the intersection of 967 and 90/41. I was at crossroads, figuratively and literally. I felt it was too early in the day to stop; I had covered only about twenty-five miles. I faced a dilemma. It looked like I might not be able to get to a place to stay for the night until very late. I had no camping gear with me, and I knew the road would be two lanes the entire way. I didn't know what the shoulder situation would be like and didn't relish the idea of bicycling for several hours in the dark. For several minutes I went back and forth about what to do; finally the pull of the Everglades was too strong.

I said a silent prayer to the bicycle gods and set off down the road. I was very excited at the prospect of seeing an alligator in the wild. There was one that lived behind Bob and Mary's house in the water hazard of the golf course they lived next to. It didn't really seem like a wild alligator, though. During my ride I scanned the water, looking for telltale eyes poking out of the water. I was almost giddy when I saw my first gator. It was soon followed by a second and then a third. I stopped counting at twenty. They were everywhere in the water. The road was elevated from the swamp; in many places the effect was like looking down from a small bridge into the water. I saw large gators, suspended, floating in the water. They hung there, motionless. It was a sight I'll never forget.

Biking through the Everglades was beyond amazing. All around me I saw alligators, large prehistoric-looking birds, and cypress trees. I stared into the landscape, transfixed. It was like being in Jurassic Park.

Much of my ride was through Native American land. At one point I passed a very large hand-painted sign that read, TELL GEORGE BUSH THIS IS NOT UNITED STATES OF AMERICAN GO BACK TO ENGLAND. Bush hadn't been president for several years.

I felt the drumbeat of the music the same time I heard it. As I closed in on the music, traffic increased. Cars were parked on both sides of the road, and people of all ages streamed out of vehicles. Young mothers, adolescents, and old, leathery, tanned men were all heading in the same direction. Local police directed auto and foot traffic. The center of the activity was a few outbuildings with a very Native American feel. I was excited to be so close to what I assumed was some sort of a cultural gathering. After I was away from the crowds, I stopped to listen to the music. It had a very familiar feel. After a few seconds, I recognized it. It was Michael Jackson's "Beat It."

The light was just starting to leave the day when I came around a slight bend in the road. I startled a very large gator, one that clearly would have no trouble making a meal of me. It slid off the opposite bank of the canal that ran parallel to the road and hit the water with a thundering boom. I was in no danger, but I did realize I wasn't at the top of the food chain in the Everglades.

I'd been right that I wouldn't make it to a place to stay for the night before dark. After the darkness settled in, I fell into a groove, and the miles flew by. I ended the day in Everglade City with a little more than eighty-three miles under my belt.

Day 121; October 20, 2010

Everglade City, Florida, to Naples, Florida—36.6 Miles

I had another flat at the start of the day. By now I had become almost an expert at changing flats. I had arranged for an overnight stay through warmshowers.org. My host was a single mother and the owner of a local bike shop. Because she had children, she didn't allow male bikers to stay at her home. She had a rental house on the canal that was vacant, so she let me have that for the night. This was my most unusual warmshowers.org stay of the trip. I never actually met my host, but the accommodations were excellent. I had a luxury home on the water all to myself.

Day 122; October 21, 2010

Naples, Florida, to Fort Myers, Florida—Thirty-Three Miles

The day started out great. The weather was ideal. My back and bum finally had stopped complaining and were back on board for the trip. My left knee, however, took off where my back and rear had left off. When I got to Fort Myers, at the thirty-three-mile mark, my left knee started to lock up. I decided I was risking injury to my knee, so I called it a day.

Day 123; October 22, 2010

Fort Myers, Florida—Rest Day

My knee still wasn't right, so I took the day off.

Day 124; October 23, 2010

Fort Myers, Florida, to Venice, Florida—56.4 Miles

I got off to a very late start. I still was having a hard time getting into a groove at the beginning of my ride. My knee, however, held up until almost the end of the day. I was hoping to be in Lutz, back with Bob and Mary, tomorrow.

Day 125; October 24, 2010

Venice, Florida, to Lutz, Florida—89.5 Miles

It was a nice, sunny, warm day—a great day on the bike. My back, butt, and knee all ganged up on me, but I was able to focus through the pain. I had to bike in the dark through some rough areas of Tampa. I got no hassles at all, which seemed to be the norm. As I entered my brother-in-law's neighborhood, however, I had the pants scared off me. A fire truck came screaming down the road behind me. It didn't have its siren on, and I didn't hear it coming. The horn blew when the truck was right behind me. The road had no shoulder; I baled off the side of the road and into the grass, my heart rate rising to record levels. I got to the house at about 10:00 p.m., just as they were closing up for the night. It was comforting to be with family again.

So far I'd racked up 336.3 miles on this leg of the trip and a little more than 2,900 miles total.

Days 126–135; October 25–November 3, 2010

Second Intermission

I stayed with Bob and Mary for the next week-and-a-half. They have many talents, not the least of which is the ability to have fun. They also have an active and imaginative social life. We listened to Radio Margaritaville while drinking beer at their tiki bar. We went to Disney World, where it felt like Bob knew every nook and cranny, every shortcut, and every bartender. Bob introduced me to multiple drinking establishments. My favorite was Cigar City Brewing's tasting room; it was dark, quiet, and filled with excellent microbrews. I only stayed with Bob and Mary for ten days, but it felt like much longer—in the best way.

My days were packed with fun, but I also was able to take stock of where I was mentally. The road had been good to me. My legs felt like iron. My cardio was almost as good as it was when I was a teenager. Mentally I was still improving. Reconnecting with family and friends was a major boon to my mental health.

I was excited to be extending my trip.

Day 135; November 3, 2010

Lutz, Florida, to Homosassa, Florida—49.5 Miles

After a great stay at Bob and Mary's, I was back on the road again. The weather was pleasant, and I had a lot of company; there were bikers on the road everywhere. One local biker I spoke to had toured with a trailer around much of Florida in the 1980s. He gave me a lot of information about bike and kayak trips in Florida. Pulling the trailer is easier on my body than carrying a backpack. I had a lot of aches and pains but nothing like the back spasms I'd suffered through in the Keys.

Day 136; November 4, 2010

Homosassa, Florida, to Fanning Springs,

Florida—64.5 Miles

I faced strong headwinds off and on all day. The temperatures were moderate, with a light intermittent rain. I had a real *Looney Tunes* moment today. I heard a clunk then a scraping noise behind me. I hit the brakes and came to a quick stop. The trailer tire flew by me, as if it had a life of its own. I actually had to chase it down the road. I was looking over my shoulder, waiting for the Roadrunner and Wile E. Coyote to show up. I'm not sure how the tire came loose, but it was able to make a run for it. After I captured it, I reattached it to the trailer and made sure it was very secure.

That night I stayed with a gentleman I had met through warmshowers.org who was about my age. He lived in a small trailer. He cooked me a great meal, and I was able to get a good night's sleep. In the morning I realized he had given up his bed to me and slept on the couch. People's generosity continued to amaze me.

Day 137; November 5, 2010
Fanning Springs, Florida, to Perry,
Florida—55.5 Miles

The road is filled with surprises. Some are good, and some are painful. Inevitably it's filled with people who touch you, people who take care of you. Sometimes when you least expect it, and need it the most, you'll find people who teach you about life. They come in all sizes, ages, shapes, colors and dentition. Some are obvious. They even advertise on sites such as warmshowers. org, like the gentleman I'd stayed with last night. They're right in front of you, and you can see them coming. Others come out of nowhere. Today I was lucky to meet yet another road angel.

I was up early after a good night's sleep. The day started off brisk, with a headwind of Mach five. It was the coldest day of the journey so far. For the first time since the start of the trip, I had to resort to wearing a sweatshirt. I made good time despite the cold and the headwind. Shortly before dark I had a disastrous mechanical failure. My rear tire had started to pull apart. The resulting gap allowed my inner tube to bulge through and rupture. I wasn't carrying a spare tire, so I attempted multiple jerry-rigs. I tried everything I could think of. Wrapping electrical tape around the tube held up for less than a mile. Cutting small pieces out of an old tube and using it to patch the gap in the tire proved futile.

I resigned myself to pushing my bike to the next town, which was twenty miles ahead. After a few miles, I heard country music blaring at ear-splitting levels ahead of me. As I neared the music, I saw a roaring bonfire behind a long chain-link fence. Also behind the fence was a collection of gentle rotting buildings perched on cracked asphalt. Scattered around the grounds was a collection of junk that would make the American Pickers salivate. A good ol' country boy and two very loud junkyard dogs greeted me. The man told me to come in, and he'd see what he could do about getting my back tire fixed. The dogs seemed medium threatening, but the man told me not to worry about either one of them. One was his, he said, and was harmless.

He told me the second one was wild but wouldn't bother me as long as I left it alone. He said the complex was the remains of an old roadside zoo.

He led me to a collection of bikes, bike parts, and tires. Unfortunately none of them fit my bike. He did have a collection of heavy-duty electrical and medical tape, which I thought might be strong enough to hold the tire together long enough for me to reach the next town. While we worked on the bike, he asked me if I wanted a beer. He said he had to drink it warm because he didn't have the teeth for cold beer. As we worked on the bike and drank warm Miller Lights, he told me about this life. Despite the ongoing ruination of his teeth, he was only in his late twenties. He lived in this compound with his mother and her boyfriend. He had been married, but his wife had passed away at a very young age. He hung his head as he told me this. He had been through some dark times after her death and had struggled with anger and drugs. In the end, he told me, he had come out the other end more or less OK. Then he said something that has always stuck with me. "You might think you're alone when you're going through bad things, but you're never really alone."

He and his mother were dirt poor, but the entire time I was with him, all he did was share everything: his beer, his food, and anything I needed to fix my bike. We managed to patch the tire with a combination of medical and electrical tape. I offered to pay for the tape, but he looked away, a little hurt, I think. He said, "I didn't help you for money."

We shook hands, and I was on my way. I left him and his world a little wiser and a little enlightened. I limped into Perry at about ten that night, tired but happy to have met another road angel.

Day 138; November 6, 2010

Perry, Florida

Despite having a great day mentally yesterday, this morning I felt tired and depressed. It was a dark day for me. I hunkered down in my motel room and slept on and off all day and night. I hate that I still have these days.

Day 139; November 7, 2010

Perry, Florida, to Lamont, Florida—30.1 Miles

My first stop was at Walmart to pick up supplies. Unfortunately they didn't have a tire that fit my bike. I patched the tire as well as I could, but I was pretty sure it wouldn't hold. I was right; the tire kept deflating, and it took me two hours to go eight miles. I gave up trying to keep air in the tire and pushed the bike for the last ten miles of the day. My pace wasn't even that of a brisk walk. I ended up camping roadside at about 10:30 p.m. It was a very taxing day. Still the night sky was clear, and the stars were beautiful. The temperature was in the thirties; it was cold, but I was in no danger of hypothermia. I'd accumulated 660 miles on this leg of the trip, for a grand total of 3,232.

Day 140; November 8, 2010

Lamont, Florida, to Midway, Florida—34.1 Miles

I had broken all of the rules of stealth camping last night. I had camped less than a stone's throw from the road—really more like a three-year-old's stone toss. My site was clearly visible from the highway. And, last but not least, I slept until well after sunrise. I walked my bike toward Tallahassee, where the closest bike shop was. On the way I had my third encounter with a road angel in less than a week. A truck pulled over; the driver was a fellow biker. He asked me if I could use a ride to a bike shop. He helped me load the bike into his truck and took me to his favorite bike shop, which was closed. Undeterred, he took me to his second-favorite shop, which was open. They tuned my bike and put on a new tire. I also added a spare tire to my arsenal of supplies and biked a few short miles down the road.

Day 141; November 9, 2010

Midway, Florida, to Marianna,

Florida—Fifty-Six Miles

The temperature was in the high sixties, perfect for biking. The sky was a gorgeous blue, and best of all, there was no evil headwind today. It was bicycling Nirvana. It also was beyond wonderful to ride all day on a newly tuned bike, with a rear tire that was full of air. The miles flew by. I crossed the Central Time Zone, another first for me on the bike. I was worried that I would cause a rip in the space-time continuum, but as far as I could ascertain, I didn't put an end to the universe.

Day 142; November 10, 2010

Marianna, Florida, to DeFuniak Springs, Florida—62.3 Miles

It was another fantastic day to bike. The weather was perfect for the second day in a row. The terrain was definitely more difficult today; I was climbing real hills but feeling terrific.

Day 143; November 11, 2010

DeFuniak Springs, Florida, to Navarre, Florida—Sixty-Five Miles

I routed myself through Air Force Land today. It was very remote, with lots of pine trees. The road reminded me very much of Vermont. It was surreal to be driving by road signs that read, HELL FIRE MISSILE TESTING RANGE—4 MILES. I was expecting to see black ops helicopters at any second. When I passed through Niceville, Florida, a small part of me thought I should stay. Living in Niceville had a nice ring to it.

That night I stayed with a friend of Bob and Mary's in Navarre, another road angel. She had a home-cooked meal and cold beers waiting for me. It was peaceful and serene to sit watching the evening news in a warm, well lit home—another thing I hope I never will take for granted again.

CHAPTER NINE

Alabama, Mississippi, and Louisiana

Day 144; November 12, 2010
Navarre, Florida, to Orange Beach, Alabama—49.5 Miles

It was another great ride today. My legs were starting to feel like iron, my body like a machine. My body hadn't felt this good since I was sixteen years old. I rode along the Gulf Coast for most of the day. There were days when I thought this would be heaven, just biking along the water for the rest of my days. I stopped at the Florida-Bamba bar, a saloon that straddles the Florida-Alabama border. It was songwriters' week at the bar, and there was music and beer everywhere. I wanted to stay, but I was afraid I might never leave. I made a mental road sign of the rest of my journey.

New Orleans: 180 miles

Baton Rouge: 260

Austin: 437

El Paso: 1,011

Phoenix: 1,400

San Diego: 1,764

Day 145; November 13, 2010

Orange Beach, Alabama, to Bayou La Batre,

Alabama—48.9 Miles

The weather was fantastic yet again today. I headed to Fort
Morgan to catch the ferry to Dauphin Island. I miscalculated
the time and arrived just as the ferry was leaving the dock, so
I settled in to wait for it to return. While I was waiting, I heard
a couple arguing very loudly. It took me a while to locate them.
They were in a car, with the windows rolled up, driving around
the parking lot. Their voices were so loud that I actually could
follow the argument. Suddenly they parked, and the woman
jumped out. He stumbled out drunk as a skunk from the driver's
side at 11:00 a.m. I had a feeling he wasn't a road angel. They
continued to snipe at each other. Then he finally rolled down to
a small bench by the water, lay down, and passed out. For the
next ninety minutes, he snored, belched, farted, and threw off
alcohol fumes at an alarming rate for the next 90 minutes. The
ferry returned and the happy couple drove onto the boat, this
time with the sober wife/girlfriend at the helm. The ferry crew
waved me on and refused my money. I love ferries.

I was enjoying the view, the water, and the sound of birds
when I heard a familiar noise—the sound of a beer being cracked
open. Mr. Not-So-Sober was loading back up for the rest of the
day. I laughed a little then cringed. How many of these drivers
had been on the road with me?

We reached Dauphin Island, and I hit the road again. The
island was very scenic, with a long bridge to get to the mainland. The darkness had covered me completely when my rear
tire went flat. In record time I changed the tire, in the dark,
almost completely by touch. I remembered how difficult and

time-consuming tube changes had been for me at the start of the trip. I finished up biking in the dark, under a beautiful moon and stars. Eventually I found an old church that proved to be a perfect camping spot for the night.

Day 146; November 14, 2010

Bayou La Batre, Alabama, to Gulfport, Mississippi—56.7 Miles

I faced a moderate headwind today, which slowed me down somewhat. I was still feeling great on the bike; my legs were becoming Incredible Hulk strong. Riding by the Gulf the last few days had been very soothing, almost Zen-like. I stayed with more friends of Bob's, Jimmy and Mernagh, two more road angels. Their house sits next to a canal off the Gulf and is in a beautiful spot at the end of a cul-de-sac. They treated me to fantastic food, conversation, and beer. What more could I ask for? I slept great—warm and snug, with a little buzz.

Day 147; November 15, 2010

Gulfport, Mississippi, to Bay St. Louis, Mississippi—23.4 Miles

I took a semi-rest day and slept until 10:00 a.m. Jimmy took me to lunch at the Blow Fly Inn. I loved the name. They had great food and, to seal the deal, a waterfront location. Jimmy also was kind enough to take me to a bike shop so I could get some equipment for my bike. There was a heavy rain in the a.m., which I sat out. I left around three. I had a short, sweet bike ride along the Gulf Coast to Bay St. Louis, Mississippi. I was very excited to hit New Orleans tomorrow.

Day 148; November 16, 2010

Bay St. Louis, Mississippi to New Orleans, Louisiana—48.1 Miles

A persistent headwind slowed me down, but I still made good time. I met another biker on tour. Ward Anderson was a sixty-four-year-old retired military man who was heading west to east. He had biked from New York to Los Angeles and now was returning from L.A. and headed to Miami. His bike was covered in gear; extra tubes dangled from the handlebars, and he was carrying water in gallon jugs. He had the look of someone who was riding on a wing and a prayer. He asked me whether I'd seen any campgrounds or motels nearby. Amazingly he was traveling without a map. I had an iPad that I checked almost compulsively for directions, while he just headed east. He told me that between his military pension and Social Security he was living the high life on the road. "I was making good time," he said, "until I discovered motels and beer." I suspect he had *rediscovered* beer; he seemed to be covering the country at the perfect pace, about twenty beers a week.

I stopped at the edge of New Orleans at the Weber Motel. The owners quizzed me about what I was doing. When I told them, they dropped the room rate to twenty dollars. It seemed like I couldn't swing a dead cat without hitting a road angel on this portion of the trip.

I'd logged 3,641 miles to date.

Day 149; November 17, 2010

New Orleans, Louisiana—8.4 Miles

I changed my route to go through New Orleans. I'd only been there twice. The first time was for a single, long, eventful day when I was in the area for hospital business. The second time was a romantic weekend with Nan. That weekend trip included a visit to the New Orleans zoo; Nan and I both loved zoos. We also spent a great night eating and drinking on Bourbon Street. That trip seems so long ago. The memory is more like a dream than something that actually happened. In fact it feels like something that happened to two people who no longer exist.

I hadn't been to New Orleans since Katrina. The hurricane had hit the city five years ago, but its aftermath was still plain to see. I passed through neighborhoods that hadn't recovered from the beatings they had taken. Seeing houses that still bore a big black X on their front doors was chilling.

I rolled into the French Quarter on Royal Street, which is immediately south of Bourbon. I stopped at the first place that served beignets. I sat on a stone wall outside the café where I bought my treats and enjoyed them and the ambience of the French Quarter. I sat there eating, getting covered in powdered sugar. As I ate, a young man stopped to look at my bike, then at me. He had a wistful expression when he spoke with me. It was a look I would wear on my face after my trip ended. "Are you on tour?" he asked, with an almost religious reverence. He talked about his experiences bike touring. He had done his riding around the Great Lakes. I acutely felt his nostalgia for the trip; he spoke of it as if it were a spiritual event. At its finest that's what a bike tour is. He told me he had to leave to meet his wife. Then he looked back at my bike longingly, as if he were gazing at an old lover he had to give up.

I thought about just blowing through New Orleans. It was early in the day, and I knew I could put a lot of miles in, but I just couldn't leave the city. So I decided to stay for a couple of days. My excuse was that I might never pass through this way again.

I found a cheap motel five blocks from Bourbon Street, close to Tulane Medical Center. I should have known I was in a different world when I checked in. Taped to the front desk was a list of rules: no hourly rates, no prostitution, no adult filming. Naively I assumed they were just making it clear that they wouldn't tolerate these activities. My first hint that I was wrong came very quickly. In the lobby I flirted with a heavily tattooed, too cute, too young girl. It was just a harmless throwaway line; I told her I was blinded by her beauty. She gave me a polite smile but no encouragements. We walked out of the lobby together. Her demeanor took a very quick right turn when we cleared the door and were in the parking lot. She was all smiles. She quickly gave me her room number and said, "Are you going to come see me?" I may be a little slow, but I was pretty sure she hadn't suddenly fallen for me. I was covered in road grime and powdered sugar, and smelled of sweat. I couldn't be mistaken for Brad Pitt without heavy medication on board. I told her politely that I would think about it.

My room was simple and surprisingly clean. If the walls could talk, I was sure they'd make a porn star blush. I showered, changed, and made the short walk to Bourbon Street. What can I tell you about my night in the French Quarter? Truthfully, not much. I will tell you that I should never be on Bourbon Street without adult supervision. I do remember buying drinks for two transvestites in a bar, having a policeman tell me to stop touching him, and spending a few cloudy hours in a "gentleman's club." I don't remember the stumble home. The next morning I woke up on the floor of my motel room. I was missing my sunglasses and a ton of postcards I had written. Somehow my wallet and credit cards were intact.

I cleaned up and attempted to retrace my steps from the night before. I drifted around for a while then located the club I had been in. When I walked in, the dancer on stage stopped dead in her tracks and screamed my name at the top of her lungs. I wasn't sure if that was a good thing, or if I was going to meet a very angry boyfriend or bouncer. She waved me over to the stage and gave me a big hug and told me how glad she was to see me. Then she said she thought I may have left some stuff there last night and I should check with the bartender. When I got to the bar, the bartender gave me a big smile. She told me she was glad to see me and handed my postcards, which she had been keeping safe for me. I was a little worried about how much money I had spent, but apparently it wasn't all that much. The dancers had a soft spot for middle-aged, depressed bikers. I had been their entertainment the night before.

Day 151; November 19, 2010

New Orleans, Louisiana, to Gonzales, Louisiana—55.5 Miles

I left New Orleans late, tired, and dehydrated from my adventures on Bourbon Street, but I felt happy. On the road I felt like I was going slowly, but I actually made very good time. The weather was cool on and off. I found it hard to leave New Orleans. The city calls to me; it calls to the adolescent that lives inside me;

it calls to the free spirit that lives inside me; and it calls to the part of me that wants to let go, to not worry about tomorrow, or the day after that, or the day after that. I thought about getting a job and staying there. It might have been the ruin of me, but it also might have been a great way to be ruined. I also met a girl there. It was the first time I had been smitten with a woman since the end of my marriage. It felt good — and scary. It was good and scary. I think it was best that I left New Orleans, but I'm not sure.

I was lonely on the road today, which was odd. I felt a lot of loneliness on the trip, but it was always at night. I really missed my kids. I missed the life I thought I had. And, truth be told, I missed Nan.

I was about two hundred miles from the Texas border.

Day 152; November 20, 2010
Gonzales, Louisiana, to Port Allen,
Louisiana—28.9 Miles

Today was a tough day. The riding was OK, but I took a nasty fall. A driver cut me off to get to his exit. He brushed by me at fifty-plus miles an hour. He was no more than six inches from me when he passed; I felt the air pushing me as he roared by. I struggled to keep control of the bike. My front tire got caught in a crack in the highway, and I lost the battle to keep myself upright. I came off the bike fast and hard. There was enough time to worry about falling in front of another car but not enough to brace myself for impact. I couldn't get my hands up and landed heavily on the right side of my chest. I was lucky that my head wasn't my first point of contact with the road. I scrambled to get up and out of traffic to avoid getting run over by passing cars. Quickly I pulled my bike and myself off the road and onto the grass. The wind had been knocked out of me, and I was shaken up.

I managed to collect myself and continued on. When I crossed the Mississippi River, I decided to call it a day. I saw a beaten-down motel and took a chance on it. My chest and right arm were becoming painful, and I craved a bed to lie down on. When

I entered the lobby, I was sure the place was closed down, waiting for demolition. The glass partition that separated the lobby from the clerk's desk was covered with the fingerprints of the thousands who had been there before me. It looked like a bizarre avant-garde art project. I started to turn to leave when I heard a tiny voice with a Middle-Eastern accent ask me if I needed a room. The voice came from perhaps the smallest grown man I'd ever met. He would have been considered small even by Hobbit standards. With very minimal expectations, I rented a room. The room was pretty nasty; it was the first time I had used my sleeping bag inside a motel. But the price was right, the TV worked, and the shower had hot water. I gulped down some ibuprofen and managed to fall asleep.

Day 153; November 21, 2010

Port Allen, Louisiana, to Simmesport,

Louisiana—59.2 Miles

My chest hurt all day. I had no trouble breathing, so I dismissed the pain as much as possible. My right arm felt moderately painful; I'd strained multiple muscles during yesterday's fall. The weather was very warm, just short of being hot. The back roads of Louisiana look a great deal like Vermont, with tons of deciduous trees. I rode on Louisiana State Route 1 for most of the day. This part of the trip reminded me of the time I'd spent on US Route 1 in New England. The road was great, with ten-foot-wide paved shoulders. That was until dark. Then the shoulder transformed into gravel and dirt. I was amazed that I had covered almost sixty miles today. At the end of the day, I felt like a warrior. In Simmesport I found the Sportsman Motel. The small motel was managed out of a convenience store/restaurant, which turned out to been a boon for me.

I realized I needed to take a couple of days off. My chest and arm weren't getting any better. The room was clean and spacious, a real upgrade from last night. I spent two days resting and eating pizza at the Sportsman. I'm sure I cracked my ribs and had a pulmonary contusion from the accident. I also had a persistent, non-productive cough that hung on for about a week. After a couple of days of rest, the pain in my chest became tolerable. My arm, however, bothered me for much longer.

The area where I was staying had very spotty cell-phone coverage. This was the first time on the trip that I hadn't been able to stay in touch with my family. I also wasn't able to update my Facebook status since the day of the accident. My daughter Erin frantically and unsuccessfully tried to find the motel where I was staying. One of the motels she made contact with told her, "Sorry. There are only women at this motel." I never did find out what the story was with that motel.

Day 155; November 23, 2010

Simmesport, Louisiana, to Lebeau,

Louisiana—Forty Miles

I stopped at the post office in Moreauville, Louisiana, to mail a few postcards. While I was outside, a woman started talking to me. She was interested in the trip, the trailer, and my story. She gave me an up-and-down discerning look, which I must have passed. Then she invited me to lunch at her goat farm. She pointed down the road and said I couldn't miss it. She said if I had trouble finding it I should just ask anyone where the goat lady lived.

I took her up on her offer. Passing up a home-cooked meal is a sign of insanity. WesMar Farms is located in a beautiful setting. The house is a sweeping, well-kept farmhouse surrounded by well-tended farmland. There was a truck parked in the driveway; people were unloading locally grown oranges and grapefruits, which they were planning to sell at their produce stand. The price for my lunch was to help them unload and bag the fruit. I happily paid it. The scene was one of moderately controlled chaos. It was hard to be sure with all the introductions, but there were at least three generations of the family, visitors from England, and many bleating baby goats.

After the work was done, we had lunch on the front lawn, underneath a stately old tree. A brightly colored, crisp, clean tablecloth covered the table. The table was laden with delicious-smelling food. My salivary glands and stomach were on high alert; I tried not to attack the food like a wild animal. I succeeded, but just by the hair of my chinny-chin-chin. I was fully satiated when I pushed myself from the table. Biking away would be a challenge with the amount of food in my belly. My lunch break had cost me several miles today, but I was very happy to have met the goat lady and her family. A light rain dripped down on me as I waved goodbye.

The overcast skies brought darkness early. I chose to bike into the night to try to make up a few miles. Fortunately the Louisiana back roads had very little traffic, and the lights of oncoming cars made it easy for me to stay out of the way of vehicles. A thick canopy of trees covered the roads. It was like being inside a very long organic tunnel.

During the ride I hit my first animal of the trip. An armadillo shot out in front of me, and I ran over its tail with my front tire. The creature made a weird strangled cry and took off like an armadillo from hell into the night.

I ended up camping just off the road. I set up my tent behind a pile of brush. After snuggling into my tent, I was full and happy. It had been a good day.

Day 156; November 24, 2010

Lebeau, Louisiana, to Ville Platte,

Louisiana—Thirty Miles

I was up early, but a strong headwind and my chest pains conspired to make it a short day. The previous night on the ground had aggravated the pain in my chest and arm. Thankfully the weather, besides the headwind, was beautiful. The temperatures were warm, and the Louisiana countryside was quickly becoming one of my favorite parts of the trip. It was the day before Thanksgiving, and I was steeling myself for a hard day mentally. In fact I planned on holing up for the day; I would keep my head down and just try to survive the day.

Day 157; November 25, 2010; Thanksgiving Day
Ville Platte, Louisiana

This was a very difficult day for me. To be away from my family on this day all but killed me.

Thanksgiving always had been a big deal for us. Nan's mother had done Thanksgiving for years. Her house actually had been too small to contain the family for several years before she gave it up. The table and chairs took up so much room that you had to go outside to get around the kitchen. The hosting of Thanksgiving eventually passed to Nan's niece Lisa (after a few of them at her nephews Jim's). It had become a monster event. Bob and Mary, as well as their kids, flew in from Florida every year. Thanksgiving seating assignments had been divided into two tables for years; the kids and the adults. Graduating to the adult table had been a much desired accomplishment. The exponential explosion in the family's population had made escape from the kids table impossible. The adult table was full, with a long waiting list. The play list was an eclectic mix that included "Alice's Restaurant" and sometimes "Grandma Got Run over by a Reindeer." The amount of alcohol consumed was staggering. There was dancing and drunken declarations of "You are my best friend" galore. The kids eventually would escape, back to Grandma's for the annual Monopoly game. "Little" Bobby (now more than six feet tall) had held a stranglehold on the game for more than a decade. My daughter, Jenny, finally had ended his reign of terror to the cheers of the rest of the players. The game had become so massive that they actually played it with two boards.

For more than two decades, Nan's family had been my family, and not being there felt like I had lost an integral part of my life. So I spent the day in my room, watching TV and dozing. I spoke with all of my daughters; it was wonderful to hear their voices but also excruciatingly painful. In the end I made my peace my making a list of the things that I was thankful for.

I was thankful for the following.

- My three wonderful daughters
- The adventure I was on
- My legs, which had taken me 3,800 miles
- Everyone who had taken me in during this trip
- My New Jersey family: Kate, Doug, and Haley
- My North Carolina family: Jess, Joel, Bradley, Lauren, and Ryan
- My Florida family: Mary, Bob, Nick, Kim, and Bobby
- Key West
- New Orleans

Day 158; November 26, 2010
Ville Platte, Louisiana, to Oberlin,
Louisiana—41.2 Miles

This was one of the most physically miserable days of the trip. It was cold, dark, and rainy. The temperatures were in the forties, but it felt much colder. I was ill prepared for this weather and was angry about my lack of forethought. I had to wear socks on my hands to keep them warm. Twice I had to stop to dry off my feet and put on fresh socks. I thought how ironic it would be to get hypothermia in Louisiana.

Despite the misery of the day, I had one of my best food experiences. I stopped at small convenience store in Mamou. The stop was more about getting warm than anything else. The smell of warm, delicious food overwhelmed me when I walked in. They sold foods that were mundane to them but exotic to me. I had my first taste of boudin there. I swear I wept tears of gastronomical delight. To discover a taste like that was amazing.

After I left the store, the misery of the day hit me full force, like a runaway train. I had covered only thirteen miles, but I declared to myself that I was done with the road for the day. I stopped at the Hotel Cazan, looking for a room. It was well before noon, and the front door was locked. I huddled in the doorway, cursing at the unfairness of the world. And then I just got over it. I hopped back on the bike and muscled through the day, finishing up in Oberlin with a respectable forty-one miles.

Day 159; November 27, 2010
Oberlin, Louisiana, to DeRidder,
Louisiana—36.2 Miles

It continued to amaze me how much of an emotional swing I could take in a day. Yesterday was pure misery. I had been ready to pack it in and call an end to the trip. Today it was a joy to bike. The road seemed to belong just to me. The rain and cold had passed and felt like a distant memory. I dialed back my mileage today, but not because I needed the rest. I just felt good and wanted to catch up on some writing and thinking. I planned to be in Texas tomorrow. It would be the first new state for me on the trip, and I was looking forward to spending time in the Lone Star State.

CHAPTER TEN

Texas

Day 160; November 28, 2010
DeRidder, Louisiana, to Kirbyville, Texas—42.3 Miles

The weather was perfect, sixty-five degrees and partially cloudy. I passed through Merryville, Louisiana, which was almost as nice as Niceville, Mississippi. As it neared dark, I came into Kirbyville and noticed a motel just as I entered town. I was intrigued by the sign out front. It simply said, MOTEL. Was it a generic motel? Vehicles, in various states of decay, were strewn around the property. Jeeps, trucks, ATVs — you name it, it was here. I had stumbled a upon the elephant graveyard of redneck transportation.

When I pulled into the parking lot, the owner walked out of the office with a Mason jar full of beer, and I knew I was home. When I asked how much a room was for the night, he looked me up and down. "How does thirty dollars sound?" he said. "I don't take credit or debit cards — cash only." Thirty dollars seemed a fair price, so I agreed. Some of the cash went into his pocket, and some went to his girlfriend, who went to the store to pick up the fixings for dinner. He must have noticed me staring at his beer, because the next words out of his mouth were "Do you want a beer?"

Three beers and two "jailhouse" tacos later, I was fast friend with the "Captain" and his girlfriend. He told me he had built the motel with his own hands, out of the cheapest materials he could find. "I built it cheap so I can rent it cheap," he said. He also was the self-proclaimed town drunk. He regaled me with stories of his many run-ins with the law. He had done some time in jail; he was a little vague about what for. Despite his outward appearance and his trouble with the police, he was well known in town as someone who could be counted to help people who were down and out. When the local churches had someone in need, they brought them to the Captain, who would put them up in his motel. His girlfriend had struggled with depression and talked openly about it. They were great hosts and made me feel very welcomed and at home.

I retired to my room with a mild buzz. The room was very plain, with no pictures on the wall, no fancy wall sconces, and no carpet. It was more like a summer-camp room. A lot of carousing was going on in the other rooms. Most of the people staying there were workers for local construction projects and were blowing off steam. I lay in bed being serenaded from the adjoining rooms. The room to my left had a couple arguing loudly in English. The room to my right offered the same, but in Spanish. I found the noise oddly comforting and fell asleep easily.

Day 161; November 29, 2010

Kirbyville, Texas, to Silsbee, Texas—32.8 Miles

Shortly after leaving the Captain and his girlfriend, I spied two bicyclists. I crossed the road to talk with them. They were two young women traveling west to east on the southern-tier route. One of them was riding a Surly long-haul trucker and pulling a B.O.B. trailer, the same model as mine. It was nice to see someone who had made the same choices I had. They had started in San Francisco and were covering about forty miles a day. They had taken the train in West Texas; they said they'd had enough of the desert. I actually was looking forward to spending time in the desert.

My first full day in Texas was medium rough. Strong head-winds slowed me down, and I started to feel like I had hit a wall. I wasn't feeling as bad as I'd felt in South Carolina, but I was feeling real slow, so I stopped early for the day. I washed my clothes, which had started to take on a life of their own. I did take some comfort in the fact that I considered a day of nearly thirty-three miles a rest day.

Day 162; November 30, 2010

Silsbee, Texas, to Cleveland, Texas—61.2 Miles

Yet again I faced strong headwinds. When the wind direction changed, it came at me hard and from the side. Late in the day, the temperature got down to a low of forty-six—not as cold as Vermont, but cold enough when biking. I got into a little groove today. Yesterday I was beat after twenty-five miles. Today I felt great, even though a flat tire on the trailer held me up. I ended up finishing the ride in the dark.

Day 163; December 1, 2010

Cleveland, Texas, to Navasota, Texas—63.4 Miles

Today was a tough day mentally. It was the twins' birthday. I remembered what it was like to see them for the first time, twenty-three years ago. Nan and I had decided that we didn't want to know the sex of the babies. We were sure from the ultrasounds that they were identical twins, but their sex was a self-imposed mystery. We struggled with what we would name them if they were boys. We both really liked the name Brendan, but "Brendan Bradley" didn't seem to flow. The twins were a planned C-section. They were transverse breech (one lying over the top of the other and both of them perpendicular to Nan's spine), which increased the chance of problems with the cords getting wrapped around one or both of their necks. Nan hadn't gone into labor and was overdue. Their estimated combined weight was fifteen pounds, and Nan was more than ready get the babies out. It was a peculiar sensation to watch someone cut Nan's belly open and then root around inside her. Dr. Dodd produced two babies out of her, like some sort of macabre magic trick. Nan was tearful; she was so happy to have the babies, but she said to me, "I wanted to give you sons." I didn't care then, or ever, about the sex of my babies. I've always been grateful for all of my girls. As I look back now, it was one of the two best days of my life; the other was the day Jenny was born. I am blessed and cursed with having a great memory; I can still see Nan's face as she lay on the table. She never looked more beautiful to me than right then.

Physically today was a great day on the bike. The wind was still in my face, but the weather was mild and very pleasant. There were more hills than I had seen in a while, but I enjoyed the climbs. The last two days it seemed that the width of the shoulder of the road was related to the amount of sunlight. When the sun went down, the shoulder disappeared. The road was very busy and very dark. At one point I spotted a police car on the other side of the highway. His light came on, and he swung around and came up behind me. I was a little leery; I was pretty sure I hadn't broken any laws, but... When he pulled me over, he was very professional and kind. He said, "I know you have every right to be here, but it's dark, and this stretch of road is dangerous. Can I give you a ride?" How could I say no to that? He gave me a ride to the lights of Navasota and dropped me off at the Comfort Inn.

Day 164; December 2, 2010

Navasota, Texas, to Brenham, Texas—Thirty Miles

The road had hills in store for me today. They were my first real climbs since Virginia, but I took my time and enjoyed myself. I stopped and took a lot of pictures and videos. The grass on the sides of the road recently had been mowed. A woman was raking and collecting the road cuttings. I stopped behind her car and asked her what she was doing. She had a world-weary look to her. She came over and told me she was gathering hay for her donkey, whose name was Opie. Her eyes lit up when she spoke of him; her love for this animal was evident. Her life had taken a hard turn several years ago. She and her husband had a farm, but it had been gradually failing, and they'd had to sell off their animals one by one. It was like they'd been forced to give up their children. Her eyes welled with tears as she spoke, and her voice wavered. Her husband had fallen into a depression and had tried to kill himself. She was caring for him and for Opie, the last of their animals. They were having a hard time keeping Opie fed.

She told me that Opie had saved her life twice. The first time was when he had refused to follow her down a path. At first she thought he was just being stubborn, but then she realized there was a rattlesnake on the path. The second time was even more dramatic. She was in a fenced-off enclosure with Opie and another donkey. The other donkey wasn't the angel that Opie was. For some obscure donkey reason, it decided to attack her. I'd always thought of donkeys as harmless; they might bite you if you put your hand near their mouth, but they're otherwise innocuous. The woman told me I was seriously mistaken. They have a powerful bite. She showed me the scar she carried; it was an ugly twisted thing, impressive in its own way. I have more than a few scars, and this one put all of mine to shame. She also told me that donkey hooves are deadly. The animal bit her leg and knocked her off her feet. She lay on the ground helplessly, certain it was going to kill her with its hooves. Opie came out of nowhere and flew over to her like a donkey from Krypton. He only lacked a cape to complete the image. Opie pinned his malevolent counterpart to the ground while the woman crawled away to safety. I was very touched by her story and her love of Opie. I pulled out a ten-dollar bill, which was all I had on me, and tried to give it to her. She was reluctant to take it. I told her it wasn't for her; it was for Opie. The woman smiled and took the money. She said she was known as the Donkey Lady, and if I needed anything while I was in the area, I should use her name.

Day 165; December 3, 2010

Brenham, Texas, to Giddings, Texas—35.7 Miles

I got an unexpected phone call. My three-year-old grandniece, Lauren, called me. Her father had let her play with his phone.

She was going through his pictures and came across one of me. She asked her father, "Where's Uncle Ed?" He dialed the phone for her, and she told me she loved me and missed me. Then she proceeded to tell me to come back—about a thousand times. She pulled very hard on my heartstrings. It was one of the best phone calls I've ever received.

My body was breaking down a little today and really needed a little rest. I planned to be with my friends Harry and Terry, near Austin, tomorrow.

Day 166; December 4, 2010

Giddings, Texas, to Manor, Texas—Forty-One Miles

I had a few Shiner Bocks last night. It wasn't a wild party night; I just had a few "relaxers." I only had a forty-mile day ahead of me and a good long rest planned for Austin; a few beers seemed more than reasonable. I left Giddings on Texas Route 290, a road that had been excellent yesterday. Today it was more like a disaster waiting to happen. The shoulder disappeared at the city limits; the speed limit spiked to seventy miles an hour, and the traffic became very heavy. An RV whizzed by me at the speed of death. I stayed on 290 for a few miles, but the traffic was too fast and too close. A station wagon with a family of kids was my next close call. I could have wiped the snotty nose of the kid in the backseat with ease.

After that close encounter of the third kind, I detoured onto secondary roads. Calling them secondary roads is being kind; some of the roads weren't much more than dirt-covered paths. They had names like Old Potato Road and were covered with gravel and lined by scrub brush. The ride was very slow going. Eventually I got back on 290 in Elgin, where the shoulder had resurfaced; it was wide and beautiful. The last few miles were a long, gradual downward hill. I flew like the wind after having spent so much of the day on cart paths. I stopped at a Sonic, gobbled down some junk food, and waited for my ride.

My old college drinking buddy Harry Linnemeyer picked me up. He showed up in a well loved, beaten-down pickup. It had a torn-up interior and dents and was covered in bruises. Harry is an oddly built human being. He stands about five-foot-four, but his arms almost reach the ground. He looks like someone cut a six-foot-tall man in half and sewed him to the bottom half of one of Snow White's friends. He also looks like he may be harboring some Neanderthal DNA lurking in his family tree. Despite his appearance and love of flannel shirts, he has a sharp, bizarre wit. He works at the University of Texas, where he manages a lab for an engineering professor. His work duties appear to be mostly terrorizing graduate students, and he's excellent at his job. His wife Terry was one of my first friends at Alfred University in Western New York. She's a beautiful, smart, confident woman who has no Neanderthal DNA in her background. I actually set Harry and Terry up on their first date; I don't think she ever forgave me. I hadn't seen either of them for a decade, but I felt at home as soon as I saw them.

Days 166–172; December 4–10, 2010

Austin, Texas, and Cedar Park, Texas—Rest Days

I spent a great week drinking beer, touring Austin, and arguing evolution and theology in Cedar Park. The simple joy of connecting with old friends was once again a powerful experience.

Day 173, December 11, 2010

Cedar Park, Texas, to Blanco, Texas—62.8 Miles

My route took me from Cedar Park down Route 620 to Bee Cave, Texas, then Route 71 to Route 3238 (Hamilton Poole Road), to Route 12, to Route 290 in Dripping Springs, and down 165 to Blanco, Texas.

It was a terrific day on the road. The weather was picture perfect, not too hot or cold. The terrain was changing. The trees were more like bushes, and cacti were beginning to dominate the landscape. West Texas appeared to have more hills than East Texas. It felt fantastic to be doing more climbing, and the bike felt great after the tune-up I got in Cedar Park. Still it was hard to leave the Linnemeyers; they felt like home to me.

Day 174; December 12, 2010

Blanco, Texas, to Kerrville, Texas—54.5 Miles

My route today was Route 102 to 437, through Sisterdale and then Comfort. In Comfort I got on Interstate 10, which I rode to Kerrville, Texas, where I finished the day.

The temperature had dropped significantly, but the weather was still great for riding. I was up and down hills all day, and an on-again, off-again wind kept my speed down. The terrain was looking a lot like the Old West. I started to look for the iconic bleached longhorn cow skull. A lot of cattle were grazing right next to the road; the cows were very interested when I stopped near their fences. I'm not sure whether they thought I was going to feed them or whether they thought my bike/trailer might be a potential girlfriend. I saw an amazing amount of diversity in the plant life; I didn't realize how many different kinds of cactus existed. Many of them reminded me of characters from Dr. Seuss books.

I found myself singing the theme song to *Gilligan's Island* all day, for no apparent reason.

It was very different to ride the interstate. If you get on the interstate on the East Coast, you can count on the police arriving within minutes, but here it was a different story. At one point I came upon a truck that a state trooper had pulled over. The trooper waved me off the shoulder and onto the highway to get around him and the truck. He told me to have a good day when I passed him. Strangely, riding on the interstate feels incredibly safe. The shoulder is as wide as the lanes vehicles travel in. The road is as straight as an arrow, which gave drivers an excellent view of me. In addition the rumble strip acts as a last safeguard. The truckers all made it a point to move over to the fast land when they passed. They also gave me a friendly toot of the horn. I was treated like a visiting dignitary. The temperature was supposed to drop to twenty-nine tonight, so I tucked myself in at a Motel 6.

Day 175; December 13, 2010
Kerrville, Texas, to Junction, Texas—54.6 Miles

I took Route 27 for the start of the day. I could have ridden I-10 the whole way, but decided to ride a back road for the day. I'd have plenty time to ride the interstate on the way to El Paso.

This morning I had another flat on the trailer. I think the Staple Fairy has been sneaking into my room at night. I also faced a ton of hills today. I resorted to my granny gear for the first time in several days. The weather was solid, with lots of sun and blue skies. The last ten miles were really difficult. My legs were doing their best to turn to rubber, and my left quad was getting tight. The song in my head today was The Carpenters' "We've Only Just Begun," but I couldn't remember any of the words except "We've only just begun," so I made up the rest of the lyrics. There's something extremely liberating about singing at the top of your lungs as you bike.

Day 176; December, 14, 2010
Junction, Texas—Rest Day

I took a rest day today; I couldn't seem to get up. My legs, especially my right quad, needed a day off. It was nice to slept late, eat, and rest.

Day 177; December 15, 2010
Junction, Texas, to Sonora, Texas—56.5 Miles

I got off the interstate and took Route 1674. The day got off to a rocky start. I had yet another flat. This time it was the bike's rear tire. I was getting very annoyed with the overwhelming number of flats and also feeling a little paranoid. I was starting to believe there was a West Texas conspiracy to drive me insane. While I was changing the tire, three truck drivers and one bicyclist stopped to check on me. The bicyclist was a gentleman in his sixties who spent some time speaking with me. He had done some touring of his own, including a ride that followed the route of Lewis and Clark.

It was very windy at the start of the day, and the road was one long, gradual climb after another. There was a single tiny town between Junction and Sonora. I biked the last twelve miles today in the dark. I still felt very safe, even biking in the dark on the interstate.

Day 178; December 16, 2010

Sonora, Texas, to Ozona, Texas—35.1 Miles

I spent the entire day on I-10. I planned a short day so I could rest and resupply for the rest of the trip. There was a great deal of open space between Ozona and the next town, Bakersfield, over 70 miles. I decided to stay two days in Ozona, which I found to be a very friendly place. I had a nagging persistent arm injury that wouldn't seem to go away.

Day 181; December 19, 2010

Ozona, Texas, to Bakersfield, Texas—71.9 Miles

I was a demon biker today; I chewed up the miles. The temperatures were mild, but there were some crosswinds and more than a few long but gradual climbs. I passed a walker today; he was resting beneath an underpass. He didn't acknowledge my passing. He was baked brown and had a hard look to him, as if he'd been through a crucible. I didn't know what his story was, but I respected his privacy. I'm not sure I could walk through the desert like he was doing. There's just so much open space out there. Today I passed no houses; at times there weren't even power lines.

It was magical to camp in the desert. The sky was clear and filled with stars. The stars were so bright and looked so close that I felt I could almost reach out and touch them. It was windy and cool but very comfortable for sleeping. I enjoyed a clear, untroubled sleep all night. The bleating of wild goats woke me at dawn. The sun rising over the desert floor was spectacular.

Day 182; December 20, 2010
Bakersfield, Texas, to Fort Stockton,
Texas—38.3 Miles

I struggled against a very strong headwind. It was hotter today but very dry. My sweat evaporated so fast that I was covered with my own salt. My clothes were stiff with all the salt that was deposited on them. By the end of the day, I looked and felt like Mr. Salty. My clothes were stiff with all the salt that was deposited on them. The plants of West Texas are fierce; everything is sharp and out to hurt you. The prickly pear cactus needles are like hardened steel, capable of piercing anything. Every plant seemed to have an evil intent for my bike and me. The plants also seemed to be able to hone in on my tires like smart bombs. If I wandered off the road, I was quickly covered in burs. I was very happy to call it a day at thirty-eight miles.

Day 183; December 21, 2010
Fort Stockton, Texas, to Balmorhea, Texas—50.4 Miles

I've nicknamed West Texas "The Big Empty." I biked almost fifty miles without seeing a house or any services. It was just me, the bike, cacti, and a few wild goats in the distance. I did an adequate job of keeping hydrated, but I did a very poor job of having enough food with me. During the last ten miles, my body went into revolt. My legs felt like rubber. My vision started to get a little dark around the edges. The worst was my stomach. My body's response to hunger isn't a pretty one. I get mild cramps followed by horrible nausea. I started to dry heave while I was riding.

When I got to the exit for Balmorhea, I all but fell off the bike. My feet and legs were cramping painfully. I lay down beside the road, in the dark, and violently dry heaved for what felt like hours. When I succeeded in getting some bile out, I knew I was in a bad way. No one passed me while I was at the edge of the road; I was on my own. I finally rallied enough to get back on

CYCLING THROUGH DEPRESSION

the bike. I pulled up to a convenience store that was less than a quarter-of-a-mile from where I had been. The store's shelves were pretty sparse. I found a few snacks but no real food. I wolfed down a Pop-Tart like I was a feral child; I may have eaten part of the wrapper. I washed it down with a Gatorade. The snack got my sugar up to a level where I could function. I checked my iPad and found what looked like a nice place to stay, the Eleven Inn.

As I biked through the town, I was taken with the Christmas lights, which seemed to be everywhere. In the middle of town, I found a store that was open and had real food. I bought a few oranges and two warm, wonderful burritos. Balmorhea is a pretty little town with a real Southwest feel. It's also blessed with an abundance of year-round water from San Solomon Springs. Balmorhea was an oasis for me on my journey through the desert. The Eleven Inn was family run. I always love to check into a motel where the family lives in the back. I could smell their dinner cooking and hear the laughter of children. With a big smile on his face, the owner came out and checked me in and gave me the lowdown on the town. Then he said that if I was staying a few days I could use their truck to explore the area. That's the kind of generosity you don't find at the big chains. The room was clean and well decorated. It also was tucked into a very quiet area. I ate my oranges and poured fluid into my body then drifted off to sleep.

Day 184; December 22, 2010

Balmorhea, Texas—Rest Day

I spent a rest day in Balmorhea. It was just such a pretty spot.

Day 185; December, 23, 2010

Balmorhea, Texas, to Van Horn, Texas—68.1 Miles

I woke up at seven, decided to doze, and woke up again at ten. I moved very slowly as I got ready for the day; I didn't leave the motel until eleven thirty. I stopped at the store and had my last two Balmorhea burritos for breakfast. I rode on I-10 the entire way today. I spotted a grand total of two gas stations in the sixty-eight miles between Balmorhea and Van Horn. I had another flat — again the rear tire of the bike. The flats had become a constant frustration; the roads of West Texas hate my tires.

Day 186; December 24, 2010; Christmas Eve
Van Horn, Texas

I had another dark day. The holidays had been very hard on me. Christmas Eve was always a big deal for our family. We always exchanged gifts and had a huge holiday feast. I was just too sad to bike today.

Day 187; December 25, 2010; Christmas Day
Van Horn, Texas, to Fort Hancock, Texas—67.9 Miles

Spending the day biking on Christmas was the best thing for me. It was hard to be on the road, but it cut down on my thinking about the life behind me. I ate Christmas dinner at a truck-stop Wendy's, my first — and I hope last — value-menu Christmas.

I had to patch my trailer-tire tube again. At this point the tube was almost more patch than rubber. I made great time for the first sixty miles, and then I had another flat. I realized that all of my bike flats had been with the rear tire. I needed to replace the rear tire and the trailer tire at the next bike store; the trailer tire was still the original tire. Near the end of the day, I crossed into the Mountain Time Zone; I hadn't known that Texas covers two time zones. So far I'd logged 4,750 total miles.

Day 188; December 26, 2010
Fort Hancock, Texas, to El Paso, Texas—43.2 Miles

I felt very strong on the bike. I only stopped around the forty-mile mark because I needed to get to a bike shop. The weather and the road were great. The truck drivers were very accommodating and friendly on I-10, waving and giving me "Shave and a Haircut" beeps. I had loved biking through Texas.

Day 189; December 27, 2010
El Paso, Texas—18.8 Miles

I ended up just biking from the east side of El Paso to the west side. The town covers a lot of miles. I also spent some time at Crazy Cats Cyclery. They set me up with an Über- tire (the Armadillo) for the rear wheel of the bikel; it's supposed to be all but indestructible. They also put in a tire saver and a slime tube.

Later that day I did a phone interview with the *Hornell Tribune*, the local newspaper in the town where I graduated from high school.

CHAPTER ELEVEN

New Mexico and Arizona

Day 190; December 28, 2010
El Paso, Texas, to Las Cruces,
New Mexico—Thirty-Nine Miles

Traveling along the Mexican border as I left El Paso was a real eye opener, figuratively and literally. The fence along the border was immense and intimidating, a presence of its own. Looking across the border into Mexico was a dramatic experience. On the US side, I passed through middle-class neighborhoods that were backed up almost right against the border. They were similar to all the middle-class neighborhoods I had biked through. They had soccer vans and nice cars in the driveways, sometimes Fisher-Price toys carelessly tossed around the yard. Maybe they had a basketball hoop or soccer goal placed strategically in the driveway. The style of the houses varied across the country, but the basic feel was remarkably similar no matter where I was. As I looked into Mexico, a few feet away, it was a different world. The houses weren't tin shacks, but the poverty was evident. The houses and streets were covered in dust and grime. Compared to the US side, it looked poor and beaten down. It's amazing what a difference a few feet can make.

West Texas was like a country of its own—a large, empty country with miles and miles of empty space. After a steep climb out of El Paso, I left I-10 and took the back roads into New Mexico. I was very excited to be in New Mexico for the first time. The plant life seemed to change quickly after I crossed the border. There were actually trees, and I passed a ton of horses. I spent quite a lot of time taking pictures and talking to the horses. No, they didn't talk back, but they were good listeners.

Outside of Las Cruces, New Mexico, I ran into two physicians who were riding very cool recumbent bikes. The bikes had a cowl that covered the bike and the rider, which made the bikes extremely aerodynamic. They told me they were capable of achieving speeds of up to thirty miles an hour! One of the doctors was particularly interested in my story and my struggle with depression. He asked how I was making ends meet. Then he reached into his pocket and pulled out two hundred dollars. He gave it to me and said, "I want you to get off the ground and stay in a hotel for a couple of nights." He was yet another road angel.

Day 191; December 29, 2010
Las Cruces, New Mexico, to Hatch,
New Mexico—Forty Miles

The weather was getting cold as I bicycled into Hatch. My Adventure Cycling map showed both a hotel and a campground. When I biked into the hotel parking lot, it was apparent that the hotel had long since given up the ghost. I roamed around looking, with no luck, for the campground. I was getting frustrated and was about to give up when I noticed something odd behind a bank—electric/water hookups for RVs. Upon further inspection I saw a scattering of old RVs and trailers. The few occupied spots looked like permanent sites. I biked behind the bank and looked for an office, but there was no apparent office. I was confused; the place looked like a campground, but there was none of the usual infrastructure. There was no office, no store, and no bathrooms; it was almost a "un-campground," a zombie campground.

Finally I knocked on the door of the most official-looking trailer, the one with the most garden gnomes in the yard. The yapping of the ubiquitous tiny trailer dog greeted me. A voice behind me called out, "I'll take care of this, Mabel." An older gentleman came out and told me the bank had purchased the campground but had allowed all the permanent residents to stay. The permanent residents, however, were gradually dwindling to nothing. He said they still allowed bikers to stay overnight. He escorted me to a fenced-off area at the back of the grounds. It looked like it may have been a playground at one point. I thanked him and started to set up for the night. While setting up the tent, I heard the sound of heavy breathing and grunting. After carefully exploring the area around my tent, I discovered my roommate for the evening. The campground was backed up against an enclosure that held a monstrous hog. He was sleeping contently, if noisily, not realizing he'd be pork chops soon.

It was getting colder. I was equipped to camp in temperatures down to around thirty degrees; if it got any lower than that, it would be uncomfortable. Tonight, in fact, wasn't comfortable. I spent some time on the Internet looking at the weather. My planned route would take me to elevations that reached nine thousand feet. The temperatures were predicted to be below zero. I made the wise decision to reroute myself; my new route would take me back south to I-10. The weather still would be cold, but I'd able to find hotels if I needed shelter. I spent the night trying to stay warm, as I listened to the wind and the breathing of the hog. The cold didn't seem to bother him at all.

Day 192; Dec. 30, 2010

Hatch, New Mexico, to Deming,

New Mexico—51.2 Miles

In the morning it was very windy. When I crawled out of my tent, it became a windsail. If not for the fence, it might have reached orbit. I stopped at a convenience store to get a quick breakfast burrito. I also invested in a knit cap and three pairs of gloves. The weather was going to be colder than what I'd been used to on the trip.

As I started out of town, a local man stopped in a beat-up pickup. He asked me where I was going. When I told him I was headed for Deming, a look of concern came over his face. He told me they were expecting a blizzard and offered to put me up for the day. I thanked him and said I thought I'd be OK. Inside I smirked a little, thinking, *I'm from Vermont. You have no idea what a blizzard is.* He did indeed did know what a blizzard was, and my smirk soon would be wiped away.

The wind was fierce and right in my face. It was so strong that I had to walk the bike up even the smallest incline; the wind was that strong. At one point I calculated that I was covering about three miles an hour. At that rate it would to take me seventeen hours to get to Deming. That, combined with the realization that there might not be anything between Hatch and Deming, made me more than a little concerned. It started to rain — a cold, miserable, driving rain that chilled me to the core almost instantly. Then the hail started; it came down painfully hard. The largest pieces were about the size of a kernel of corn. I pulled over and huddled behind a very small sign for whatever protection it could give me. If the hail got much bigger, my plan was to set up my tent and wrap myself in my sleeping bag and clothes and ride out the storm. Mercifully the hail didn't last long, but the temperature suddenly plummeted, and it started to snow. The snow was thick, wet, and heavy and clung to me like a second coat. I looked like an Arctic explorer, with a frozen beard, ice crystals in my mustache, and a thick layer of snow covering my gear. I was wearing almost every piece of clothing I had with me. Two T-shirts, a riding jersey, a sweatshirt, a rain jacket, a knit cap, riding shorts, sweatpants, three pairs of gloves, and three pairs of socks kept me from completely freezing.

I pushed on; I really had no other choice. The road was very quiet. After I was a few miles out of Hatch, I didn't see any more cars on the road. Suddenly the wind changed direction; it was still bitterly cold, but I was able to make better time. My feet got very cold and then numb; ice had begun to form inside my shoes. Eventually I came upon an RV parked a little ways off the road. Using it to protect myself from the wind, I stripped off my wet, freezing socks and put on my last three pairs of dry socks. I checked my toes for signs of frostbite; they still looked healthy and whole. The RV was locked and empty.

I pushed on again. The weather teased me a few times. The sun would come out and warm me up a little; then it would disappear behind some clouds, and the temperature would plunge. I rode into Deming after dark. I was definitely suffering from the early stages of hypothermia. My shaking had been coming on strong for some time, and I found it hard to concentrate. At the outskirts of town, I stopped at the first gas station/ convenience store I came to. When I entered the store, the heat felt blissful.

The Google map on my iPad directed me to a Motel 6 less than two miles from the station. After a quick ride—almost a sprint—I was at the location. The location, to my dismay, was an empty lot. My map had failed me. I could see a Comfort Inn and several other hotels a short distance from the non-location of the Motel 6. I decided I'd pay whatever I had to get out of the cold. When I got to the front desk at the Comfort Inn, they had some bad news for me. They were sold out. In fact they told me they thought all the hotels in town were sold out. Didn't I know that all the roads, including the interstate, were closed due to the weather? The light bulb finally went on over my head. That was why I'd had the road all to myself. I asked them about the Motel 6. They told me it was on the other side of town, about five miles. I got the number from the front desk and gave them a call. Fortunately they had a few rooms left. I begged them to hold one for me, so that I wouldn't freeze to death, and they agreed to save one for me. After a quick ride to the opposite end of town and a quick check-in, I finally was in a warm and toasty room.

Days 193–194; December 31, 2010–January 1, 2011;
New Year's Eve and New Year's Day
Deming, New Mexico—Rest Days

New Year's Eve and New Year's Day were just too cold to bike. I holed up at the Motel 6 for a couple of days, waiting for better weather. I treated myself to a steak dinner and a couple of bourbon and Cokes on New Year's Eve at the Holiday Inn.

Day 195; January 2, 2011
Deming, New Mexico, to Lordsburg,
New Mexico—62.8 Miles

The weather was fairly cold but OK for riding. There was no wind, which was great. I stayed on I-10 the whole way. I made really good time, in part because it was too cold to stop and also because there was nowhere for me to stop. I was really in the big wide open. At one point I crossed the Continental Divide. I found myself singing the old America song "A Horse with No Name" as Bob Dylan. Any song is cooler if you sing it as Bobby, even "I Got a Brand New Pair of Roller Skates."

I stayed in a motel that night. It was way too cold to even think about sleeping in my tent. The owner checked me in. Some of the most interesting people I met on the trip were motel owners. This particular owner was an American classic. He was standing behind a cluttered front desk. It was hard to say how old he was. A lifetime of smoking and working outdoors had left his face filled with crags, creases, and a valley or two. He wore a cowboy hat and looked the part of an old-time ranch hand, but he called himself a redneck hippy, with a wink. He left no doubt in my mind that he had smoked his share of weed in his formative years. He told me he had been a millionaire several times; he said he'd also been dead broke several times. He looked and talked like someone you'd see guarding the Mexican border, but he spoke with pride about sneaking his third wife across the Rio Grande in an inflatable raft.

In short he was a person whose life couldn't be placed into a neat category. He was proudly a round peg that had found its way into a square hole. I found it fascinating to listen to him; he was better than free cable.

Today I crossed the five-thousand-mile mark.

Days 196–197; January 3–4, 2011

Lordsburg, New Mexico (Whining Alert)

I woke up with a headache, the first in forever. Despite having rested two days in Deming, I was still tired. I'm not sure if it was the weather, the altitude, or just the toll of being on the road, but I just couldn't bike today. I decided to wallow, eat, and watch TNT all day. The next day it was more of the same.

Day 198; January 5, 2011

Lordsburg, New Mexico, to Wilcox,

Arizona—73.5 Miles

The weather was cold in the morning—thirty-five degrees or so; eventually it warmed up to around fifty. There were lots of gentle but long climbs on my ride today. There also was snow on the ground and on the tops of the mountains in the distance. I spent the entire day on I-10.

Today I crossed into Arizona, my next-to-last state for the trip.

Day 199; January 6, 2011

Wilcox, Arizona, to Benson, Arizona—39.5 Miles

I slept late and great. The weather was warmer; I picked up fluids at Family Dollar and headed out. Again I spent the entire day on I-10 (or "the 10," as the locals call it); I climbed the whole day. It wasn't a big grade, but it was constant all day. It turned hot at the end of the day; it was nice to finally be warm. At one point I passed the exit for Tombstone. I thought about taking a side trip, but it was twenty-four miles in the "wrong" direction. In retrospect I wish I had made the detour.

Day 200; January 7, 2011

Benson, Arizona—Rest Day

I wasn't sure if it was the elevation or the toll of seven months on the road, but I couldn't bike today.

Day 201; January 8, 2011

Benson, Arizona, to Tucson,

Arizona—Forty-Four Miles

Today was a very odd day. It started with a long, steady climb out of Benson. Later in the day, the road leveled out, and I made good time. The weather was sunny and warm but not too hot. I was planning on calling it an early day in Tucson. The NFL playoffs were today. I'm not a diehard football fan, but watching a playoff game with my feet propped up and a beer in my hand sounded great. I entered Tucson in the early afternoon. Two teenage boys, maybe fourteen or fifteen years old, biked up behind me. At this point I'd had nothing but great interactions with the people I'd met. One of the boys pulled up and said, "How you doing, Chewbacca?" Inside I laughed; to be fair it was a pretty accurate statement. I hadn't cut my hair or trimmed my beard since October 12 in Tampa. The second boy started to bump my trailer tire with the front tire of his bike. I told him to knock it off. The first boy told me, "BIke faster," then yelled to his friend, "Grab his flag." The flag on my trailer had become my prized position. It had the signatures of a multitude of people I had met on the trip— everyone from the Captain, to Bob and Mary, to the goat lady. The boys had crossed a line. In a heartbeat they had gone from harmless kids to street punks. I slammed on my brakes and jumped off my bike then did my best completely-deranged-lunatic-on-a-bike impression. I flailed my arms, cursed and screamed incoherently. I did it so well that even I believed it. The two amigos had been cocky wanna-be thugs. They quickly turned into "holy crap; we're just a couple of punks, and he's going to kill us and eat us" babies. They pedaled away as fast as they could to find their mommies. After they were out of sight, I laughed and laughed.

My next interaction with a Tucson native took place about two blocks later. An angry man in a dust-covered pickup yelled out his window, "Go back to Mexico!" I was starting to wonder if stopping in Tucson was a good idea. I decided to take my chances and checked into a Motel 6. I turned on the TV as soon as I entered the room. On the TV was a special news story. I had hit Tucson on the day that US Representative Gabrielle Giffords had been shot. I was stunned. To have arrived in Tucson on this day was almost too bizarre for me to believe.

Day 202; January 9, 2011

Tucson, Arizona, to Eloy, Arizona—46.4 Miles

The day started wonderfully. The road was a joy to be on, and the weather was almost perfect. A Dairy Queen yelled—no, *screamed*—at me as I approached it. I couldn't resist its Siren-like call. After feasting I came out of the restaurant to find a flat rear tire on the bike, which was very frustrating. In El Paso I had purchased the tire of tires—a tire that laughs at flats, a tire so strong that it's suspected that sorcery is involved in its manufacturing. I also had bought tire savers and a self-sealing tube. All of these, however, were in vain; the tire was flat. It had succumbed to a tiny puncture that it should have just ignored.

I patched the tube and limped into Eloy, Arizona. I was beat. I know some of it was mental; the flats were getting the best of me. I was looking forward to a few days' rest in Scottsdale, with Cindy, my sister-in-law's sister.

Day 203; January 9, 2011

Eloy, Arizona—Ten Miles

It wasn't a good day for me. I couldn't get the tube patched, and I was out of tubes. I pushed the bike for ten miles. Then I spotted a Motel 6; they had left the light on for me. I pushed my bike into the lobby and checked in. In the room I took a long, hot shower that I sorely needed, both for my mental health and to wash the dust of the road off me. After the shower I searched the Internet for the closest bike shop, or at least a Walmart. Sadly I was fifteen miles from the closest tube. I called Cindy and asked her if she could pick me up. Thankfully she said she could.

Day 204; January 10, 2011

Eloy, Arizona, to Scottsdale,

Arizona—by Car, Fifty Miles

I was in the shower when the lights went out in the room. I toweled off and went to the lobby. The owner was there and returned with me to the room. He was very apologetic. He couldn't get the power back on in my room. All the other rooms were fine; it was just mine that was dead. He offered me another room while I waited for my ride, but I told him as long as I could keep my gear in the room until Cindy got there, all would be fine. I hung out in the lobby while I waited and talked with the owner. He was from Pakistan and had come to the United States and found success in the motel/real estate world. He was very proud to be an American. He spoke with pride about how much this country had given him and how much it meant to him. He told me how he had felt on 9/11. After that horrific day, he had gathered a group Pakistani businessmen like himself. He told them this country had been very good to them, and it was time to pay her back. He had passed the proverbial hat for donations for the relief effort and was rewarded with an outpouring of goodwill and resources. He wept as he told me the story. I felt like I had met a true American hero.

Cindy arrived around one o'clock. We packed the bike and my gear in the trunk and backseat of her car and were off to the magical land of Scottsdale.

Days 204–208; January 10–14, 2011

Scottsdale, Arizona—Rest Days

I rested in the comfort of Cindy and Bob's home in Scottsdale. The days passed quickly. My mind and body were in an odd flux. They needed rest, but they couldn't seem to get it. I slept for hours and hours, but I was still tired. I wanted to move on, but I also wanted to stay. All of Mary's relatives were incredibly generous and kind to me. The impending end of the trip weighed heavily on my mind; I knew it was almost time to end this journey. The frightening part was that I didn't know what would come next.

Day 208; January 14, 2011

Scottsdale, Arizona, to Casa Grande,

Arizona—51.1 Miles

After a few very restful days in Scottsdale, I thought I was ready to get back on the road. I wasn't it turned out. I did some last-minute adjustments, said my goodbyes, and pulled away. There was no wind in my face; the weather was fantastic; and the roads were a dream to bike on. I was excited to be getting closer and closer to San Diego. I had gotten a late start, so I biked in the dark for a while. I love biking in the dark. If it weren't so dangerous, I'd do it all the time. The moon was beautiful and bright, and the sky was clear and full of stars. Visibility was excellent. I felt good but also a little sad. The night was one that was meant to be shared with someone you loved.

Days 208–212; January 14–18, 2011

Casa Grande, Arizona

I'm not sure what hit me. I was enveloped in depression, all but paralyzed. I just lay around in a motel doing nothing. Was it a reaction to last night's beautiful star-filled sky? The pain of not having anyone to share the night with? The realization that Nan was thousands of miles away from me, both physically and emotionally? I really don't know the answer; I only know I was dead in the water. I was a sailing ship of an bygone era. There was no wind in my sail, no current to move me. I was at rest but not resting. It was very discouraging to be so depressed this late in the trip. I felt like an abject failure. I battened down the hatches, watched reruns of *Law & Order*, and prayed for a breeze to come and lift me.

Day 213; January 19, 2011
Casa Grande, Arizona, to Gila Bend, Arizona—65.7 Miles

I had a hard time getting started. My depression was lifting, but it wasn't gone. Once I got started, it was an excellent day on the bike. One of my tires, however, lost air at the twenty-mile mark. I used my new toy, a CO_2 inflator I had purchased in Scottsdale. The tire inflated like magic. I wanted to go back in time and stupid-slap myself for not starting the trip with one. On 1-10 I traveled a couple of miles, when a police officer stopped me. The stretch I was on was apparently off limits to bicyclists. They made me walk my bike a couple of hundred yards to I-8, which I rode the rest of the day to Gila Bend. One of the officers gave me my first written warning; I felt like a real outlaw biker.

A short while later, I had to change the front-tire tube. It had held up since Austin, Texas. The weather was splendid. I felt like I was moving at a slow pace, but I made good time. My arms, however, especially my right one, were very stiff and sore. At one point I had a real Forrest Gump moment. The land flattened out; the road stretched out forever; my beard and hair were out of control; and I could almost see the people following me. At the sixty-mile mark, I hit a very nice climb—not really what I was hoping for, but I made it. The sunsets in the desert are very cool, different than in the east. I had to bike a little after dark. The stars were out, and everything felt very serene.

Day 216; January 22, 2011
Gila Bend, Arizona to Wellton, Arizona—90.6 Miles

I rode a little more than ninety miles today, a new record. It was just a long, wonderful day. With the Southwest scenery and blue skies, I felt like I could bike forever.

Day 218; January 24, 2011

Wellton, Arizona, to Yuma, Arizona—20.1 Miles

As I neared the end of the trip, I was having a very hard time. I felt like a giant invisible hand was holding on to me, pushing me back into bed when I tried to get up. It took all I had to get out of bed and on the bike. Twenty miles seemed like an intergalactic rip; I was dead on my feet. I finally did get on the bike but faced strong winds and very long, steep climbs before I reached Yuma, Arizona. Then I called it an early day to catch some football games on TV. I treated myself to a steak, two hurricanes, and strawberry cheesecake at a local bar.

Day 219; January 25, 2011

Yuma, Arizona—10.8 Miles

All I did today was ride from the east side of Yuma to the west side. I got a little shaky; perhaps it had something to do with my blood sugar. I stopped at a Motel 6 after my short trip across town. Both of my tires were soft. I went to Mr. B's Bicycles & Fitness to do something about the tire issue. They had a two-year flat guarantee posted on the wall. They guaranteed that I'd have no flats for two years if I let them do their magic. At this point I was ready to try anything. They put in two super-duper tubes and two extra-strong flat stoppers, and filled the tubes with slime. I passed the time talking with Mr. B, the owner. It turned out he was from Drum, Pennsylvania, about two feet from Hazleton, Pennsylvania, where I was born.

CHAPTER TWELVE

California

Day 223; January 29, 2011
Yuma, Arizona, to El Centro, California—Sixty Miles

I finally left Yuma, where I had spent five days. I couldn't bring myself to cross the border. Nan and I always had wanted to go to San Diego. The first year we were married, I was fifteen minutes from buying plane tickets there for our first Valentine's Day as husband and wife. I clearly remember thinking we'd have plenty of time to take the trip later. The trip never happened, and I still regret not buying the tickets. What had held me up in Yuma for the past few days was the finality of the loss of that dream. It felt like I should be going to San Diego with Nan; once I crossed the border into California, that dream would be dead. I knew that wasn't a completely rational thought process, but I had come to realize that I wasn't the completely rational person I'd thought I was before the trip.

I got zero sleep last night; I couldn't stop the noise in my head. Sleep always has been fairly elusive for me. Last night it ran away and hid. I got started early, but the day almost ended on the first mile. I had a wicked cramp above my right knee; I thought I had pulled a muscle. I managed to work the cramp out, however, with a little stretching and massage.

I finally was in the magical land of California. This was my first time in California and my first time in the Pacific Time Zone. When I crossed into California, the desert was astounding. I saw sand dunes everywhere; I'd never seen anything like it before. A caravan led by camels wouldn't have looked out of place here. Still the modern world was apparent; dune buggies were scooting around the desert. They looked like an enormous amount of fun.

The landscape changed dramatically fifty miles into California. The dunes faded away. Green fields and palm trees dominated the landscape, and the cacti began to disappear. My first day in California was a success and a real joy.

Day 224; January 30, 2011

El Centro, California, to Ocotillo,

California—27.9 Miles

I had to fight for every foot today. The wind was brutal. The sand blew painfully into my face and made visibility very difficult. Bicycle traffic was banned from this stretch of I-8, so I took a detour onto County Road 80, which was very torn up and slowed me down. I'd be able to get back on I-8 tomorrow. I had less than one hundred miles before I hit San Diego. I felt the end of the trip stalking me, but not in a bad way.

Day 225; January 31, 2011

Ocotillo, California, to Jacumba,

California—Nineteen Miles

I had a sit-down breakfast before I started for the day. The owner of the restaurant said, "I hear you're going up *the grade* today." Word really travels fast in small towns. The awe in his voice should have tipped me off that it would be a tough day. At the first switchback, I noticed a cement cistern that was marked, NOT FIT

FOR HUMAN CONSUMPTION. I would come to hate that sign. The road was one switchback after another, and I felt like I was going up forever. Halfway through the ascent, I met several Sherpas who had turned back. It was an awesome climb, but I had made a major fluid miscalculation. I had more than enough fluid for the nineteen miles it would take me to get Jacumba—more than enough if I hadn't had to climb all day. The grade soon depleted me of my fluid, and the going got very tough the last few miles.

When I got to Jacumba, I was dry as a bone. As I rode up to the Jacumba Hot Springs Hotel, three men drinking beer on the patio cheered me on and welcomed me like I was a returning war hero. They wanted me to stay and drink, but I told them I had to get rehydrated. After checking in I made my way to a convenience store and purchased as much Gatorade as I could carry. Back in the room, I drank my fill. I had every intention of joining my three amigos, but my body decided it wasn't going anywhere.

Day 226; February 1, 2011

Jacumba, California, to Pine Valley,

California—Twenty-Nine Miles

Today was filled with solid climbs. My legs felt very heavy, and my body had had just about enough.

The twenty-nine miles felt like ninety. That night I stayed in the mountain village of Pine Valley. Tomorrow I would be San Diego, the last stop on my journey. I was happy and sad simultaneously. The trip had been an epic experience.

Day 227; February 2, 2011

Pine Valley, California, to San Diego,

California—Forty-Seven Miles

It was cold in the morning, with temperatures in mid-thirties and wind gusts of up to thirty miles an hour. After an initial steep climb, I started on a downward hill, which lasted ten miles. It was the longest descent of my bicycling career. It was amazing how fast those miles flew by. Then I did a short stint on I-8. The crosswinds were fierce, and the temperatures increased as I went down.

It was bright and sunny as I entered San Diego. All my fatigue, pain, and depression fell away. I felt pure joy to have reached the end of my journey.

I wanna take your boat as far as it goes, feel Jamaican sand between my toes.
I wanna ride on the wind just as far as I can.
I won't be any trouble to haul… I can sleep anywhere at all.
And I don't eat very much for a hollow man.
I wanna ride on the wind just as far as I can.

I had ridden the wind as far as I could.

CHAPTER THIRTEEN

The Aftermath

I had covered 5600 miles and passed through twenty-one states. The trip had come to an end. I felt elated, sad, exhausted, proud, and a little scared. It had been my life for more than seven months, but it seemed like so much longer. I felt like I had spent my entire life on the road. What else was there? I had hoped I would have clarity at the end of the trip; I had hoped I would have acquired knowledge and wisdom as to what the rest of my life should be. But that wasn't to be. Did I acquire knowledge? Yes, I had filled my head with knowledge: how to change a bike flat, how to pitch my tent in the dark, how to keep hydrated, how to use food as fuel, what West Baltimore was like, what sunset was like in the Florida Keys, what New Orleans was like after dark, how much pain I could withstand, what my physical limits were. I had learned all of that and more. I had learned to depend on myself, how to take care of myself physically and mentally. I had learned that we never lose real friends; they're just waiting for us around the next bend in the road of life. I learned that the world is a big beautiful place.

Did I gain wisdom? I think so. I would like to humbly share that wisdom with those who have persevered through this book and my travels.

For me depression is a chronic condition. I can treat it, but it's always there. It will, I fear, always be waiting. It always will lurk in the darkest part of my brain, in the labyrinth of my mind, waiting to throw its black tentacles around me. It waits. It waits to pull me to its lightless, painful, comfortless breast. But I learned that depression doesn't define who I am. It doesn't have to be the controlling factor of my life. I know that no matter how deep I fall, I have the ability to climb out of the pit. I learned — really learned — that I can do anything. I define who I am — not the depression. And it doesn't define who you are either.

I learned that you can transform your life, even at the ripe old age of fifty-three. If you aren't happy, then change. Go on a journey, whether it's physical or metaphysical. Whether it's around the block or around the world, get your head and feet moving. Will you find what you're looking for? Maybe…maybe not. But I guarantee that you will find something. You will find something new, something worth knowing, something worth the pain of the journey.

Watch for me. I'm just ahead, around the next bend.